YOU AND YOUR TENANCY

Other Books in the Need2Know Series

A full list of books can be obtained from

Need2Know, 1-2 Wainman Road, Woodston, Peterborough PE2 7BU

Help Yourself to a Job
Step by step into work
Jackie Lewis

Buying a House
Ease the path to your new front door
John Docker

Stretch your Money
Get more for your £££'s
Michael Herschell

Make the Most of Retirement
Live your new life to the full
Mike Mogano

Make the Most of Being a Carer
A practical guide to lightening the load
Ann Whitfield

Breaking Up
Live your new life to the full
Chris West

Successful Writing
The beginner's guide to selling your work
Teresa McCuaig

Superwoman
A practical guide for working mothers
Marion Jayawardene

Work for Yourself and Win
A practical guide to successful self-employment
Ian Gretton

The Expatriate Experience
A practical guide to successful relocation
Bobby Meyer

Forget the Fear of Food
A positive approach to healthy eating
Dr Christine Fenn

Improving your Lifestyle
Live a more satisfying life
Mike Mogano

Forthcoming Books:
Safe as Houses - Security and Safety in the Home
Everything you Need2Know About Sex - The A-Z Guide to Increase your Knowledge
Travel Without Tears - An Essential Guide to Happy Family Holidays
Prime Time Mothers - A Positive Approach to Delayed Maternity
Parenting Teenagers - Make the Most of this Unique Relationship
Planning a Wedding - A Step by Step Guide to the Happy Day
Improving Family Life - A Guide to Getting Along
A Guide to Bereavement - A Sympathetic Guide to the Road of Recovery
Women and the Change - Step by Step through the Menopause
Get What you Pay for - A Guide to Consumer Rights
Take a Career Break - Bringing Up Children Without Giving Up your Future

Need2Know

YOU AND YOUR TENANCY

A Helpful Guide to Feeling at Home

Sue Dyson

Need2Know

ISBN 1 86144 011 1

First published by Need2Know, 1-2 Wainman Road,
Woodston, Peterborough, Cambridgeshire PE2 7BU
Tel 01733 390801 Fax 01733 230751

Edited by Kerrie Pateman
Design by Spencer Hart
Typesetting by Forward Press Ltd

Contents

Introduction

Surviving as a tenant is a very serious business.

I know this because I have been a tenant for the last eight years. Selling my own home after a divorce, followed by six house-moves in quick succession, made buying a property out of the question.

Just to make matters worse, being self-employed made it difficult to get a mortgage. The only answer was to become a tenant - something I hadn't been since my student days.

For renting to work really well (and it can work), it needs to be an amicable partnership between landlord and tenant; unfortunately it is sometimes more like a battle of wills. The problems you may face can range from losing your deposit to being blamed for damage you haven't caused; from arguments about noise, pets or children to harassment and unlawful eviction. When problems do arise it's hard not to feel frightened and alone, especially if you don't know where you stand.

You and Your Tenancy looks at some of the most common questions that tenants ask, and offers a combination of information, anecdotes and suggestions for solving everyday problems.

Disclaimer

This book is definitely *not* a substitute for proper professional and legal advice. The fact is that I'm not a housing expert, just a fellow tenant who has experienced a few of the problems at first-hand.

You and Your Tenancy is designed as a short, user-friendly guide for anyone who's thinking about moving into rented accommodation. It offers practical, sympathetic and (hopefully) sensible advice, but it's not a statement of the law. If you have serious problems, you *must* consult a solicitor, housing advice centre, social security office, law centre or Citizens' Advice Bureau.

NB: *You and Your Tenancy* concentrates on renting property in England and Wales. The Scottish legal system is quite different and deserves a book of its own.

In the course of the book the landlord and tenant are often referred to as 'he' for the sake of clarity and brevity; but no gender bias is intended or implied.

1

The rented sector is definitely expanding, after years of decline. More and more people are becoming tenants, particularly in the private sector - either through private landlords, agencies or housing associations. Many have turned to renting not through necessity, but through choice.

But why? Why would anyone in their right mind want to be a tenant?

What kind of people become tenants?

The short answer is, 'all kinds of people'. Gone are the days when tenants consisted of students, the elderly and the poor. Nowadays, with the stagnant housing market and recent changes in the law, more and more properties are becoming available to rent - and that means that more people are becoming first-time landlords, too.

The housing market

The mid-1980s saw a massive boom in house prices and sales, particularly in the South-East, with everyone scrambling desperately to buy something, anything, before prices soared out of their reach. A few people made huge profits, others bought over-priced properties which later turned out to be brick-built disaster zones.

As we all know, boom turned to slump and the housing market has been virtually stagnant for several years now. Negative equity has made it impossible for many home-owners to sell, even though they need to move house.

If you can't sell your house, you may be able to rent it out. This is something which an increasing number of people have discovered. Many lettings agencies offer a full property management service, collecting (and in some cases guaranteeing) rent in return for a percentage of the income from the property.

Provided they are consulted first, many mortgage lenders look sympathetically on this kind of situation, and the creation of assured shorthold tenancies makes it much easier for a landlord toensure he obtains immediate repossession of his property when the tenancy expires.

The government have also introduced a 'Rent-A-Room' scheme, which encourages home owners to take in lodgers, in return for income tax concessions. This, too, can be a lifeline for anyone who owns property and is in financial difficulties.

Mark and Shakhira bought their house in 1988. Within six months its value had plummeted and they had to put several thousand pounds into the property to pay for structural repairs. When Mark's firm relocated to the North-West, they wondered what they could possibly do. They couldn't afford to sell their house, and in any case nobody was interested in buying. In the end they placed their home with a lettings agency, which found suitable tenants, collected the rent and took care of maintenance. Mark and Shakhira were able to afford to rent an unfurnished property up north, and are currently landlords and tenants.

Relocation

With job insecurity and widespread redundancy, workers are having to be more flexible - and mobile - than ever before. It's rare for anyone to stick with the same job or firm for the whole of their working life, and in many cases keeping in work means moving all over the country. Firms are also relocating, particularly out of London and into other cities. In some cases placements are temporary, and it makes little sense to buy property even if you can manage to sell your existing home.

Dagmar works as a staff trainer for a large national company. She often has to spend several months at a time at the company's branches, which are spread out across the country. Her company doesn't provide accommodation, but subsidises her and helps her to obtain short tenancies through agencies in the areas where she is working.

Relationship problems

When relationships break down, the distress felt on all sides is only increased if one or both partners have to leave the family home. Often renting is the only option, if the property can't be sold or there isn't sufficient equity to buy two properties when everything has been split up.

Marco and Diane's marriage hadn't been good for a long time. In the end they agreed that it would be best if they split up, and Marco moved out, leaving Diane in the family home with their two young children. He wanted to maintain contact with his family, and also worked locally, so he found a flat to rent on the other side of town. This gave him and Diane the space they needed to work out their problems. When Marco had financial problems, his landlord was able to release him early from his tenancy agreement, and he moved into a cheaper property for a few months, before eventually moving back home.

Getting a mortgage

Mortgages are harder to get than they used to be. Lenders are much more cautious about who they lend to, and also about the amount of money they are prepared to lend. This forces more people into rented accommodation, at least until they are able to save up enough money for a substantial deposit.

Certain people have always found it difficult to get a mortgage: for example self-employed people, undischarged bankrupts, anyone with a history of debt, anyone who has had their home repossessed, unemployed people and those on low incomes or short-term contracts.

When you add to this the fact that property is now a less attractive investment than it used to be, it's not surprising that so many people are looking for rented accommodation.

Kaoru wanted to buy a flat, but when she approached her building society she was turned down for a mortgage because they required three years' audited accounts and she had only been running her business for two years. She took an assured shorthold tenancy for a fixed term of twelve months, and was able to buy a property the following year.

Reasons to be cheerful

Being a tenant isn't all gloom and doom, by any means. Renting has some definite advantages over home ownership. For example:

- renting allows you to be pretty mobile. At the most, an assured shorthold tenancy will commit you to six months in one place, whereas if you own a house you have absolutely no idea how long it will take you to sell up - or if you will recoup the cost
- renting allows you to react quite quickly to changes in your circumstances. You can move to a cheaper or dearer property, according to changes in your position
- renting allows you to plan your expenditure. Most repairs and maintenance are likely to be your landlord's responsibility, whereas (as every home-owner knows) owning a property is a never-ending round of bills, bills and more bills

On the other hand...

True, there are some less attractive aspects to being a tenant. With recent changes in legislation, it is now difficult to find private rented property which carries any security of tenure. Landlords are not always good landlords (any more than tenants are always model tenants), and if you are unlucky you may suffer minor harassment or worse.

If you're a lodger you will probably have very little protection under the law, and we've all heard horror stories of people coming back 'home' to find all their possessions have been thrown into the front garden...

There are also the less tangible annoyances, such as the uncomfortable feeling of living in somebody else's house, surrounded by somebody else's furniture and somebody else's taste in wallpaper. Not to mention the monthly inspections, when some official from the lettings agency finds fault with your dusting.

But don't let anyone tell you that being a tenant is all bad. Ask any harassed home-owner with a crippling mortgage, a leaking roof and ten thousand pounds' worth of negative equity.

2

The world of renting is quite a complicated one, and it pays to know where you stand. As explained in the introduction, this book is only intended as a general guide, not a statement of the law - but in this chapter we take a brief look at some of the different types of tenancy you may encounter when you start looking for rented accommodation.

Are you a tenant?

Not all letting agreements can be defined as tenancies. Some are more properly called 'licences', which are not covered by the same legal provisions.

A tenancy is an arrangment by which exclusive possession of a property is granted for a fixed or ascertainable period of time. In return, the tenant usually (although not necessarily) pays rent to the landlord.

There are two key elements which define the arrangement as a tenancy:

- 'fixed or ascertainable time': the tenancy agreement should state when your tenancy starts and how or when it will end

- 'exclusive possession': if you only have the right to share the accommodation (eg if you're lodging with the owner of the property), and don't have exclusive use of any part of the property, then the agreement is a licence rather than a tenancy. 'Exclusive possession' means that you can exclude other people, including your landlord, from the premises

Finding out whether or not you are a tenant is important, as tenants have more protection under thelaw than licensees. For example, if you are a licensee and your landlord decides to sell the property,your licence probably won't be binding on the new owner and you may not be allowed to stay on. You have less protection against eviction than a tenant, and no security of tenure.

It can be difficult to decide whether an agreement is a licence or a joint tenancy - for example, if a group of people are sharing a house. Landlords may prefer to think of them as licensees, as they will have fewer rights and be easier to get rid of, but (depending on the nature of the agreement) a court might see them as tenants. It is very important to draw up a written agreement, with professional guidance wherever possible.

What the law says

Tenancies are governed by a number of housing laws and the rules can be difficult to decipher. If you're not sure which sort of tenancy (or licence) applies to you, it's important to seek professional advice and clarify your position at the outset - don't wait until problems arise, because by then it could be too late.

If in doubt, don't sign anything until you're sure you understand what you're committing yourself to.

The main pieces of legislation are:

- *Housing Act 1985* covers most local authority tenancies and some other public sector lettings. These are called 'secure' tenancies. Housing association tenancies created before 15 January 1989 are usually regarded as public sector tenancies, but as private sector tenancies if created on or after that date
- *Rent Act 1977* covers most private sector tenancies granted before15 January 1989. These are called 'protected' or 'statutory' tenancies
- *Housing Act 1988* covers most private sector tenancies created since 15 January 1989. These are called 'assured' or 'assured shorthold' tenancies, and we shall be concentrating primarily on these types of tenancy, as they are now the most common form of private sector tenancy agreement

The type of tenancy you enter into will affect two very important aspects of your life as a tenant:

- security of tenure (your right to remain in the property)
- rent control (your right to question the amount of rent you are asked to pay)

Types of tenancy - the private sector

Tenancies under the Rent Act 1977

Most tenancies created before 15 January 1989 come under the Rent Act.

Security of tenure

Good. Your landlord can only regain possession of the property by establishing a 'ground for possession' and obtaining a court order.

Rent

These tenancies come under the 'fair rent' system, which tends to keep rents lower than the market level. A local authority rent officer will assess your rent and decide the maximum amount which can be paid. If you've been overcharged, you can claim back up to two years' overpayments.

You can apply for a fair rent assessment at any time, and the level decided stays in force for at least two years except in exceptional circumstances.

Passing on your tenancy

If you die, your partner will succeed to the tenancy if s/he was living with you at the time of your death. This doesn't apply to same-sex partners.

Assured tenancies

Most private sector tenancies created on or after 15 January 1989 are assured tenancies. Even if you don't have a written tenancy agreement, your tenancy may be an assured one if you have made a verbal agreement.

The property let must be for residential use (not an office), and must be a single dwelling, not several units occupied by several different people. The tenant must have the right to exclusive occupation of at least one room, or the agreement is a licence rather than a tenancy. If facilities are shared with the landlord, the tenancy is not an assured one.

Security of tenure

At the end of your tenancy you have a right to stay on as a statutory periodic tenant, except in the case of a court order or an agreement between landlord and tenant.

The landlord can only get you out by proving a valid ground for obtaining possession, and so obtaining a court order. The grounds for this are listed in the Housing Act, and include such things as failing to pay rent or the landlord wishing to regain possession of the property in order to live in it as his main home. Some grounds are mandatory, others discretionary.

The property must be your only or principal home. If this stops being the case, your tenancy may cease to be an assured one (temporary absences such as holidays don't count).

Rent

There's no restriction on the amount of rent which can be charged when the agreement is drawn up - it's fixed between landlord and tenant, according to market levels. But your landlord must follow the correct procedure if he wishes to raise the rent. This procedure is usually written into the tenancy agreement.

If you have a periodic (week by week or month by month) tenancy, your landlord must serve notice on you, indicating the amount of rent he wants to charge. You can refer this to a local rent assessment tribunal, who will decide the proper market rent.

Subletting

This is usually forbidden by being written into the tenancy agreement. Otherwise, you might have the right to sublet, take in lodgers or assign your tenancy to someone else.

Passing on your tenancy

If you die, any survivors of a joint tenancy will succeed to it. If you're a sole tenant, it will pass to whoever is named in your will. Your spouse or partner will automatically succeed to the tenancy if s/he has been living in the property with you, as his/her principal home, prior to your death - but this doesn't apply to same-sex partners.

Some kinds of tenancy cannot be assured. These include:

- tenancies created before the 1988 Housing Act
- business tenancies

- lettings to students by universities and colleges (not private lettings)
- holiday lettings
- lettings where there is a resident landlord (these usually have no security of tenure, and not much protection against eviction)

Assured shorthold tenancies

These are fixed-term tenancies of not less than six months' duration, with no security of tenure and not much rent control.

Most private tenancies created since 15 January 1989 are assured shortholds. Landlords love them, because once they expire the landlord has a right to regain possession, provided the proper procedures are followed - this means that you will almost certainly be given a possession notice before you sign the tenancy agreement, warning you of the landlord's intention to recover possession.

Security of tenure

There isn't any.

At the end of the shorthold, you can stay in the property as a statutory periodic tenant (ie week by week or month by month), but you still have no security of tenure - though the landlord must give you at least two months' notice that he wishes to regain possession.

On the plus side, the landlord cannot regain possession during the initial six months - you're entitled to stay until the shorthold expires.

Rent control

Not much. You can refer the rent to a rent assessment committee, but they will only reduce it if it is 'significantly higher' than market levels for similar properties in your area.

In theory you can leave the property at any time, but you are committed to paying rent for the full six months - unless you have a very sympathetic landlord who will release you (say, if you manage to find someone suitable to take over the tenancy).

The 'Rent-a-Room' Scheme

This is a scheme set up by the Government to encourage home-owners to take in lodgers. It applies to resident landlords.

Generally speaking, the income from property rentals is liable to income tax. However, under this scheme, the rent your landlord receives from you is exempt from income tax as long as it doesn't exceed £3,250 per year.

The rules are quite complicated, and it might be worth your while to obtain a copy of the leaflet which has been prepared for the guidance of prospective landlords (you should be able to get this from your local Inland Revenue office).

Public sector tenancies

Local authority (and some housing association) tenancies are covered by the Housing Act 1985. They are called 'secure' tenancies, and have:

- good security of tenure
- succession rights if the tenant dies
- no rent control

Landlords may be local authorities, an urban development corporation, new town corporation or a similar authority.

Security of tenure

Your landlord can't end your secure tenancy except by obtaining a court order for possession. At the end of a fixed-term secure tenancy, you may be able to stay on as a periodic tenant. Most council tenancies are periodic tenancies.

The Housing Act 1985 lists the grounds under which your landlord may apply for a possession order.

Passing on your tenancy

If you die, your partner will succeed to your secure tenancy, if s/he was living with you at the time of your death. If you have no partner, a member of your family who was living with you for at least 12 months prior to your death can succeed to the tenancy.

You can't transfer your tenancy to another person, except:

- if you die (succession rights)
- in an exchange with another secure tenant
- in a property adjustment order (matrimonial proceedings)

Subletting

You can take in lodgers, but you must not sublet without your landlord's written consent.

Rent control

There isn't any. But the landlord can only increase your rent if the tenancy agreement says so. In a periodic tenancy, your landlord must give you at least four weeks' notice of any rent increase. You have no right of appeal.

Housing association tenancies

Housing associations have greatly increased in number over recent years. They are non profit-making bodies set up and run by management committees of volunteers. Paid staff may be employed, but the committee is responsible for running the association.

More than two million people currently live in housing association homes throughout England, and around 35-40,000 new homes are developed each year. Homes are either offered at an 'affordable' rent, or sometimes for sale on a shared ownership basis, to people who could not otherwise afford to become home-owners.

Housing association tenants vary widely, and include people with disabilities, single parents, low income families, and vulnerable residents such as the young, the elderly and people who have recently left long-term institutions.

Tenants may be nominated to a housing association by their local authority, or by a specialist agency. Tenancies created before 15 January 1989 are dealt with differently from those created on or after that date. Most housing association tenants are now assured tenants, under the 1988 Housing Act. It is important that you check the legal rules which apply to your particular tenancy: most recent ones are regarded as being in the private sector, most earlier ones as being in the public sector - but the rules are complex.

Registered Housing Associations

Some housing associations are registered with the Housing Corporation or Housing for Wales, which fund and supervise their activities. Some are also registered as charities, with their own internal system to regulate their behaviour.

Registered housing associations must provide their tenants with a written agreement, setting out the conditions of the tenancy and the level of rent payable. They will also provide a 'tenant's guarantee'.

This sets out the tenant's minimum rights and gives information about how the association operates. The Housing Association Ombudsman can act on behalf of tenants who have a grievance against a housing association which is registered with the Housing Corporation.

Unregistered Housing Associations

These don't qualify for state funding and are not supervised by a public body. Registered associations can't set up shared-ownership schemes, which is why some associations prefer not to be registered. No 'tenant's guarantee' is given.

Co-operative Housing Associations

These have their own co-operative constitutions, and the tenants are their own 'landlords'. For recent tenancies, the 'tenant's guarantee' applies, stating that rents must be affordable by tenants on low incomes.

Furnished or unfurnished?

As far as rent control and security of tenure are concerned, the law doesn't make any distinction between furnished or unfurnished lettings.

However, if you're thinking of taking a furnished or part-furnished property, you should be aware of recent regulations. The *Furniture* (Fire) (Safety) *Regulations 1988* state that upholstery, fillings and covers must comply with specified flammability tests.

There are certain exceptions to these rules, and also other regulations with which landlords must comply: these are discussed in Chapter 6 (Rights and Obligations).

Summing up

Although the Assured Shorthold is now the most popular and prevalent form of private tenancy, you may encounter many different types of agreement.

It's very important to know what you're dealing with before you sign your rights away, so don't be afraid to ask questions - and get professional advice if you're in doubt. Don't rely on verbal agreements, even if you're planning to rent a property from family or friends. Misunderstandings can turn into major disputes, and it's far better to get things sorted out at the outset.

Don't be intimidated by the landlord who tells you 'not to worry' about the details of the tenancy agreement, or to 'leave everything to me'.

Don't be afraid to question or negotiate when you're looking for a place to live. A good landlord will respect your need to know and protect your rights.

3

So - you're looking for a place to rent. But before you put pen to contract, take a few minutes to think: are you absolutely sure you know what you're looking for?

Silly as it may sound, people do sometimes end up renting properties which aren't really what they wanted, and mistakes can be expensive both in money and time. Remember, if you sign up for an assured shorthold tenancy, you will be committed to paying at least six months' worth of rent, so if you can afford to, it is well worth pausing before you commit yourself. In fact, can you afford not to?

Mistakes can happen for a number of reasons:

- Pressure from the landlord or agency to 'make up your mind quickly, there are lots of other people after this place, you know' (even if there aren't)
- The need to find somewhere quickly (and the fear of ending up with nowhere to live)
- Choosing a place on the strength of one very brief viewing
- A lack of thought about what you really need

The persuaders

Your future home may be rented: but it is still your home. Isn't it worth taking the time to choose wisely?

Don't let landlords or agents persuade you to take a property against your better judgement. It's in their interests to 'sell' you the property, even if it's unsuitable for you. The agency is chasing a fat commission, and the landlord may be in deep trouble with negative equity, desperate to find someone to take on the mortgage payments. If at all possible, hang on to your money until you're sure you have found a home where you'll be comfortable and happy.

Here are some of the questions you need to ask yourself.

Furnished or unfurnished?

A rented property may be advertised as furnished, unfurnished or part-furnished.

The number of unfurnished and part-furnished properties is on the increase, owing to recent fire safety regulations regarding soft furnishings. Rather than go to the expense of buying brand-new three-piece suites and mattresses, many landlords are choosing to take out the furniture and advertise the property as 'part furnished'. A part-furnished property may include as little as a cooker and a carpet, or almost an entire house-full of furniture. Even unfurnished properties usually come complete with a cooker, and perhaps a fridge and/or washing machine.

Contrary to what you might expect, you won't pay any less rent on an unfurnished property than you would if the same property was furnished. Landlords may be reluctant to remove their furniture to allow you to move in your own goods and chattels - leaving you with the choice of either giving up the property or living with two lots of everything. At one property I rented, I found myself squeezed in with no fewer than four dining room tables!

Not infrequently, you will meet the landlord who suspects everyone and everything, and who is determined to impose special conditions on you as a matter of principle. If you have children or pets, or if you are a smoker, this will almost certainly be the case. For example, you may have to agree to have the carpets and curtains professionally cleaned on departure (no matter how filthy they were to begin with). Professional carpet and upholstery cleaning can work out pretty expensive (over £100 to clean a house-full of carpets), so if this is in your contract, budget for it from the start.

At one property, I discovered that the landlord had removed some of the furniture between the signature of the tenancy agreement and my moving in - apparently because the furniture was 'nice' and he was worried that my two cats would damage it. It is important to take note of what is in the property before you sign the agreement, and confirm (if possible in writing) what is to stay and what - if anything - will be removed.

Occasionally, a landlord will agree to take all the furniture out of a furnished property and put it into storage for the duration of your tenancy, and this can make all the difference if you have a house-full of possessions and can't afford the cost of storing them until you move on.

If you have children or pets, and the property contains items which are antique, fragile or valuable, you may wish to ask the landlord to remove them for your own peace of mind. It can be nerve-wracking trying to reconcile three boisterous toddlers and an Alsatian with a priceless Chippendale.

Should you have your own furniture and appliances, remember that it can be very expensive to store everything for six months or a year. If you have to move into furnished accommodation, you may find it works out cheapest to rent a property with a garage or extra room, into which you can put all your possessions until you move on.

How much is it going to cost?

To a large extent, the type of property you choose will be dictated by the price you can afford to pay for it. Remember that council tax and water bills are frequently not included in the monthly rent, and you will usually be directly responsible for settling these bills.

Check to see if there is a water meter in the property - if you have a young family, you may find that your water bills will add considerably to your monthly outgoings.

If you are currently receiving benefits or are on a low income, check to see if your entitlement will be affected by a move to rented property. Can you obtain any additional help?

If you feel that the amount of rent being asked is unreasonably high, you may have the right to appeal to a rent tribunal, which has the power to alter the amount payable in certain circumstances. Your right to do this will depend on the type of tenancy you are taking out.

When you think you've found somewhere, add up all your income and outgoings and make sure that you can afford the property you are interested in. Remember that once you are in the property, you are committed to paying rent on it until your tenancy agreement comes to an end - and being in debt is no fun for anyone. What's more, being in arrears with your rent could end up losing you your home.

Location

Try to view the property in daylight. It is very difficult to assess either the property or the location after dark.

Is the property close to any amenities (eg schools, shops, public transport)? Is it likely to be noisy? What are the neighbours like? One property I viewed seemed ideal... until I realised that it backed onto the local Unigate depot, with its chorus of clanking milkbottles and milkfloats at four o'clock every morning!

If the property has a garden, is it your sole responsibility, or do you share it with your neighbours? Who is responsible for its upkeep? What sort of condition is it in - and will you be expected to pay towards the cost of a professional gardening service?

If the rent seems very low for the size and quality of the property, this could be an indication that the property is considered to be in a 'poor' area. A very high rent may suggest that your chosen area is considered fashionable, but it may not be a 'better' area in terms of safety or amenities.

Bear in mind that if you are renting in an area rated as a high crime risk, you will have to pay more in premiums for household contents insurance. Insurance companies base their premiums on postcodes, and their lists are a good indicator of which are considered to be the safer and 'better' areas to live in.

Special conditions

You will also wish to investigate any special conditions imposed by the landlord or agency. These can range from the prudent to the extremely bizarre.

Inspections

One common example is the inspection. Inspections may take place at regular intervals, or on an ad-hoc basis: one reputable national agency carries out inspections every three months, another uses occasional maintenance calls as an opportunity to check out the property informally. Some don't bother you at all, as long as you pay the rent on time.

In themselves, inspections aren't a bad idea. They enable the landlord or managing agent to keep an eye on the property, and also give the tenant an opportunity to point out any problems which need dealing with. This can be especially useful if you've been badgering your landlord for months to carry out some repair or other, and so far nothing has been done.

In practice inspections are frankly a pain in the backside; although a lot depends on the spirit in which they're carried out, and the amount of notice you are given. It can be absolutely horrible to have your home invaded at the drop of a hat by a Nazi with a clipboard, intent on finding fault with everything from your choice of loo-brush to some imaginary new stain on the lino. So if the idea of regular inspections really bothers you, check this out before you move in - lots of perfectly reputable agencies don't bother with them.

Foibles

There's no accounting for tastes, and some landlords have peculiar ideas which they expect tenants to carry out to the letter. Sometimes this works to the advantage of the tenant, sometimes not.

For example, a friend of mine and his wife were desperate to find cheap accommodation in South London. In the end, they happened upon a middle-aged widow who was offering a self-contained flat for only £25 per week (a tiny amount even then). It sounded wonderful... but there was a catch. In return for this peppercorn rent, my friend and his wife had to agree to display the landlady's paintings - several dozen of them - all over the walls of the flat. In addition, she was to be allowed to come and look at them whenever she wanted.

This wouldn't have been too bad if the paintings had been restful landscapes; but they were lurid abstracts in dayglo orange, scarlet and electric blue. Nevertheless, my friends were in no position to argue and they did eventually take the flat. In fact, they lived there quite happily for several years, hiding the paintings under dust sheets and bringing them out whenever the landlady paid them a visit!

Other special conditions might include taking care of a tankful of tropical fish or selection of exotic plants. If you can face the dreadful possibility that they might all die on you, then proceed... but with caution! That unbelievably low rent may conceal a hidden catch.

The property itself

It's quite likely that you will see a property only once before you sign the contract - so make the most of that initial viewing.

Pay attention to details

As with the general location, it is always best to view the property in daylight if at all possible. It's amazing how unforgiving natural light is - the cracks in the walls and the stains on the carpets really show up.

If you come across defects which are perhaps not immediately obvious (eg a hole in a carpet covered by a table or chair), make a mental note to draw them to the landlord's attention when you are working through the check-in inventory. If you don't mention them as soon as you move in, you may be liable to pay for their repair when you move out... and in one extreme case I heard about, this meant shelling out for an entire room's worth of fitted carpet.

Ask yourself if you'd be happy in the property. Does it feel cosy, welcoming? If not, is there anything you could do to it to improve it - and would the landlord object if you redecorated at your own expense? Does the property have all the facilities you need? Is it warm, light and airy - or cold and draughty? Does it have central heating - and if so, what kind? Is the property spacious, or cramped? Is it suitable for your children?

You'll also wish to check out the safety aspects of the property, and consider installing smoke alarms yourself if these aren't already fitted. You can also purchase inexpensive carbon monoxide indicators which you can place next to gas appliances if you have doubts about their safety (although it's worth pointing out here that landlords are obliged by law to have these professionally checked and maintained at regular intervals).

Be aware that there can be some real horrors. A friend moved into a small flat where the bath was situated in the middle of the kitchen. It was months before he discovered that if he had a bath when the cooker was switched on, he was in danger of being electrocuted...

From the horse's mouth

One of the best ways to find out about a property is to talk to the current tenants. Generally speaking, tenants have no particular axe to grind. They are unlikely to have any interest in deceiving you - unlike an unscrupulous landlord or agency, who may well be prepared to bend the truth in order to hook a new tenant.

Of course, it's especially important to meet the current tenants if you are thinking of renting a room in a shared house. No matter how nice the house is, your life will be total misery if you can't get on with your future house-mates. And if you don't like the look of them the first time you meet, you probably won't get on with them any better when you're living on top of each other, seven days a week.

Think out your questions before you visit the property. These might include:

- How do you get on with your landlord/the agency?
- Are you left pretty much to your own devices, or are there regular (unannounced) visits by your landlord orrepresentatives from the agency?
- Have you had any problems with the property (eg faulty electrics, gas appliances, structural or plumbing problems)?
- Are there any defects which need putting right?
- Have you received a prompt response in dealing with these problems, or is the landlord/agency reluctant to undertake routine maintenance?
- Have gas appliances been checked recently by a CORGI registered installer? (under recent legislation, landlords are obliged to check gas appliances for safety at least once every twelve months)
- Is the property safe and secure? (eg is it fitted with smoke alarms, window locks?)
- Is the property expensive to run: what are the monthly bills like?
- What are the neighbours like? And the area? (if you don't know the area at all, the current tenants can be a mine of useful information about schools, shops, buses etc)

Getting what you want

Few properties are perfect. You're incredibly lucky if you manage to get everything you want, at aprice you can afford.

But even if the property you choose isn't ideal, remember that there is often room for manoeuvre. If there is something you particularly want (or don't want), try negotiating withyour prospective landlord. Issues worth talking about include:

- *Furniture* Your landlord may be willing to consider removing or replacing certain items from the property on request
- *Safety* Don't settle for anything you know is unsafe. Be aware of your landlord's legal obligation to provide a safe living environment for you (see Chapter 6: Rights and Obligations)
- *Rent* If you genuinely believe that the rent being asked is too high, it may be possible to refer the matter to a rent tribunal. (But remember that renting privately is generally more expensive than paying the equivalent mortgage for a similar property)
- *Special clauses* For example, if your lease specifies that you must pay for a professional gardening service, but you are a keen gardener, you may be able to negotiate a rent reduction in return for keeping the gardens tidy yourself
- *Duration of tenancy* By law, an assured shorthold tenancy must be for an initial period of at least six months. If you are keen to have a flexible agreement, you may be able to arrange for a month-by-month or week-by-week rental agreement after an initial six-month lease
- *Pets* Frequently, a prospective landlord will specify 'No Pets'. This may be because of previous bad experiences with carpet-chewing dogs or incontinent hamsters, and of course landlords have every right to safeguard their property. It's up to you to persuade the landlord that your pet is different.

  If you're pretty certain that your pet won't do any damage, it's worth seeing if there's any room for negotiation. A landlord who hates dogs may accept a couple of cats, and vice versa. Be honest about your pets... but be prepared to sign a clause specifying that you will be responsible for any damage, and will have carpets etc professionally cleaned before you move out
- *Condition of the property* If you know that there are serious defects in the property, eg plumbing problems, you may be able to put pressure on the landlord to rectify them before you move in

There may, of course, be many other issues on which there is room for negotiation, so play it by ear and be prepared to be as flexible as you want your landlord to be.

But remember: if you do come to any agreements, it is advisable to formalise them in writing. I once agreed with a landlord that he would provide a sofa for my living room. Unfortunately we made only a verbal agreement... and six months later, I was still waiting for a sofa which never arrived.

Summing up

Be realistic. Don't demand perfection - but do be prepared to hold out for the things which are most important to you. Landlords and lettings agencies may regard you as a necessary inconvenience, but they need your money; and that money gives you a certain power.

Checklist

- Tenancy or licence?
- Type of tenancy
- Length of tenancy: six months, twelve? Option to extend?
- Location
- Local amenities
- Size of property
- Condition of property
- Any defects which need rectifying?
- Shared or sole use of facilities?
- House or flatmates?
- Rent
- Monthly bills
- Council Tax
- Water bills
- Service charge, gardening costs etc
- Any special clauses written into contract?
- Private landlord or agency?
- Absentee landlord, or on premises?
- Safety and security

4

So you've decided to take the plunge.

You've found a place you like, at the right price. You've viewed it, asked the right questions, and feel you could be happy there. Now it's time to say yes, and draw up the tenancy agreement... but what exactly are you saying yes to?

In this chapter, we take a look at the stages you will need to go through before you actually get the key to the front door of your new home. Although (as we saw in Chapter 2), there are many different types of tenancy in the marketplace, the most common form of private tenancy nowadays is the Assured Shorthold, and this is what we shall be concentrating on in this chapter.

Your landlord

When you sign a tenancy agreement, you're not just committing yourself to a property: you and your landlord are also committing yourselves to each other. Your prospective landlord will probably spend lots of time and energy checking you out, so why shouldn't you think hard about your landlord's suitability, too?

Private landlords

If you are thinking about taking out a licence as a lodger, or a tenancy in a property with a resident landlord, it's particularly important to think about whether you are going to get on.

I once lodged in a house owned by a man who had recently divorced. He had used all his savings to buy the biggest house he could afford, at the height of the 1980s' housing boom. He then discovered that the house had serious structural problems, and the only way he could afford the mortgage and the repairs was to fill the house with lodgers.

Through a friend, he arranged to take in three French students, two girls and a boy. He had never met any of them until the day they turned up on his doorstep. It took about five minutes for them all to decide that they loathed the sight of each other, and over a year for him to save up enough money to manage without them. The house echoed to tantrums, screaming rows and graphic threats - from both sides. Nobody had a very good time, although one of the French girls did get her revenge by running up an enormous telephone bill.

Obviously it's difficult to be absolutely sure about your landlord before you move in, but it makes sense to meet up a couple of times before you commit yourself. If there are other tenants/licensees already in the property, chat to them and see if you can spot any warning signs or potential problems which could be solved before you sign up.

Agencies

If you'd rather somebody else took care of the formalities, you may prefer to obtain accommodation through an agency.

Again, proceed with caution! Lettings agencies (sometimes called property management agencies) vary greatly in quality, integrity and the fees they charge. There are some really excellent agencies out there, but there are some terrible ones too - so be sure that you can spot the signs.

Some agencies belong to professional bodies, and these may give some indication of quality service. However, they don't give guarantees or very much protection, for that matter - although it might be embarrassing for them for any shortcomings to be made public.

The main organisation specifically covering residential lettings is ARLA (the Association of Residential Letting Agents), but reputable agencies may also belong to ISVA (the Incorporated Society of Valuers and Auctioneers), NAEA (the National Association of Estate Agents) and RICS (the Royal Institution of Chartered Surveyors).

Agencies charge fees to landlords for finding tenants and managing their properties. These fees can start at 10% of the tenant's rent, with extra to pay if the landlord wants a full management service.

One sure-fire way to spot a dodgy agency is if it tries to get money out of *you*: reputable agents do not charge tenants a signing-on fee, or charge them for lists of accommodation (though you will have to pay a fee for 'drawing up the tenancy agreement').

The best way to choose a lettings agency is to visit all the agencies which cover the area you're interested in, and also ask as many people as you can for their personal recommendations.

You should also compare rents between the various agencies (and private advertisements). Is the rent you are being asked for reasonable for the property you have chosen?

Reserving your property

Once you have decided on a property, you may be asked for an initial deposit to 'reserve' it in your name until all the formalities have been completed. This amount should be subtracted from the security deposit which you will be asked to pay on commencement of the tenancy, and will prevent the property from being offered to anyone else. Note that if you later change your mind and withdraw, you may forfeit the initial deposit you have paid.

Forms, forms and more forms

It's at this point that you begin to realise just how complicated things can get. It's rarely a case of handing over your money and moving straight into your new home.

The formalities involved in applying for your tenancy can be quite long-winded and may even take a week or two. In some cases, eg if you need somewhere to live very quickly, it may be possible to speed things up, but landlords - and especially lettings agents - will need certain information about you before they agree to grant you a tenancy.

Character references

Unless they already know you well, landlords will ask you to provide a character reference. This means giving the landlord the details of someone who knows you (an employer, a doctor, priest, teacher etc) and who can comment on your good character, reliability and suitability as a tenant.

Clearly that landlord needs to be sure that the new tenant is the sort of person who will respect and look after the property, and not cause any trouble.

Check that your referee knows that s/he is about to be asked for a reference, and is happy to provide one.

Financial references and credit checks

Just as important as your personal qualities is your ability to pay the rent! The landlord's main aim in letting property is to make money, and this means finding a tenant who can and will pay.

Some evidence of your income will be required. You could be asked to supply payslips or bank statements, or to give the name and address of your bank and sign a form stating that the bank may disclose details of your financial status to the landlord or agency. Usually, the agency will write to the bank, asking if you are capable of paying a specified sum of rent per month, rather than asking for fulldetails of the amount in your bank account.

Credit checks

If you're applying to an agency, your financial references will almost certainly be backed up with credit checks, using agencies who can advise on the credit-worthiness of just about anybody. They carry a great deal of personal information, including such details as debts, county court judgements, bankruptcies etc.

If you have been refused credit in the past, you may find it difficult to obtain a tenancy. In some cases it is possible to see and check your credit record, to ensure that it does not include any false information - people have sometimes been wrongly blacklisted.

If you are turned down and can't understand why, it is worth asking. A mistake may have been made.

Self-employed?

If you are self-employed, providing references can be a bit of a headache. In addition to providing a bank reference, you may be asked to give the name and address of your accountant or bookkeeper, if you have one. It is often more difficult for self-employed people to obtain rented accommodation, just as it is for them to obtain mortgages, particularly if work is intermittent and there are wide fluctuations in monthly income.

No job?

If you are unemployed or on a low income, you may be entitled to assistance via housing benefit - your local housing advice centre can provide information.

In some cases, a landlord will require you to provide a guarantor - someone who will sign the tenancy agreement on your behalf, promising to meet the rent if you fail to do so. This may be the case if you are a student or have only just obtained your first job, or possibly if you don't have a bank account.

The landlord or agency will take up references to checkthat the person who has volunteered is an acceptable guarantor.

Mortgagee's consent

One question which you must ask before signing the tenancy agreement is: is there a mortgage on the property?

If the landlord has a mortgage, he must ask the bank or building society for permission before he lets out the property. If he doesn't and defaults on the mortgage, the lender has the right to take possession and sell the house to get back the money owing to it. This could result in you, the hapless tenant, losing your home; so if you're entering into a private arrangement with a landlord, make sure you know where you stand on this. If you're using an agency, ask if there are any safeguards to protect you.

Paying the rent

Some landlords and agencies will be happy for you to pay your rent by cheque or cash, but increasingly they are asking tenants to set up standing order or direct debit mandates, so that the rent is paid automatically from your account each week, month or quarter.

You will be asked to fill in a form with details of your bank or building society current account - note that non-cheque book accounts may not offer a direct debit facility, so you'll need to check this out.

The security deposit

When you sign the tenancy agreement, you will be asked to pay a security deposit - either in cash or a bank/building society cheque. If you pay by personal cheque several days will have to elapse for the cheque to clear before you can take possession of the property.

The sum of money you pay on signature will normally represent a specified amount of rent in advance (eg one month), plus the security deposit. There are no hard and fast rules about how much the security deposit should be, but it is often the equivalent of one month's rent - although I have been asked for one and a half or even two months' rent.

This is obviously a substantial amount of money, and you need to be certain that you can raise it - and manage without it until the end of the tenancy. The deposit provides security for the landlord. He holds it against damage, bills or non-payment of rent. At the end of the tenancy it should be returned to you, less any deductions eg for damage or cleaning, or for payment of outstanding bills. However, there are often disputes over the deposit; so it is important to check your inventory carefully on entering the property, and to establish from day one what you may be liable for when your tenancy ends.

In some cases your deposit will be held in a building society account, and will actually gain interest for you.

The prescribed shorthold notice

Before you sign an assured shorthold tenancy agreement, your landlord should give you a prescribed notice, warning you what you are entering into and making it clear that s/he may be entitled to regain possession at the end of the initial six-month period.

The tenancy agreement

Unless you want to make trouble for yourself, don't rely on an informal, word-of-mouth agreement. You owe it to yourself - and your landlord - to insist on a proper written tenancy agreement. If your prospective landlord is a friend or family member, it is very tempting to dispense with the formalities and stick to a verbal agreement. In point of fact, agreements between friends are often the most problematic of all, *so don't do it.* Discuss what you both want from the arrangement and put it in writing, preferably in a document drawn up by a solicitor or on a pre-printed form (available from a legal stationer's). You should both sign and date the agreement, and each keep a copy.

Remember that the law lays down certain rules about tenancies and licences, and it may not be possible for an agreement to override these legal rights and obligations, even if you both agree to the terms. If in doubt, get professional advice.

Whatever method you choose, there are certain areas which your agreement should cover, in order to avoid future problems:

- The property: the tenancy agreement should incorporate a description of the property and its contents. The landlord should also draw up an inventory listing everything in the property, and the condition of each item. You should have an opportunity to comment on this inventory and make any necessary amendments to it before signing and returning it. This will be referred to at the end of your tenancy, when the cost of any damage etc is assessed and deducted from your security deposit

- Duration of the agreement: If you are taking out an assured shorthold tenancy, your agreement will give a commencement date and state the length of the tenancy (not less than six months)
- Type of tenancy: assured? assured shorthold? or other?
- Rent: how much rent you will pay, and how often. What will happen if there are any rent arrears (eg will they be deducted from the deposit? Will interest be charged on arrears?). Any provisions for increasing the rent (eg if water charges are included in the rent and these go up)
- Deposit: how soon after the end of your tenancy will it be returned to you? What deductions may be made?
- Tenant's obligations: how the property is to be used, and your obligation to keep it in a good condition etc. Any important prohibitions, eg subletting, children, pets, assignment of the tenancy to anyone else
- Repairs: who is responsible for what?
- Insurance: your landlord will normally insure the property, but you mustn't do anything which might cause the policy to become void, or anything which might cause the premium to be increased
- Access: a statement of the landlord's right to give notice of any need to enter the property to undertake repairs or inspections
- Landlord's (or agent's) address: for service of any legal papers
- Break clause: any break clause can only come into effect after the first six months if this is an assured shorthold tenancy
- Forfeiture of the tenancy: you may forfeit your tenancy if you fail to fulfil the obligations set out in the agreement
- Mandatory grounds for possession: grounds under which your landlord may apply for a court order to regain possession of the property
- Water bills: these are usually paid by the tenant, unless otherwise stated
- Council Tax: usually paid by the tenant, except in cases of multiple occupancy

- Stamp Duty: you will be charged for this. It will be based on the amount of rent payable annually on the property
- Dates and signatures: of landlord and tenant, signed in presence of witnesses

Summing up

Landlords and agencies vary greatly; check them out before you commit yourself. Talk to other tenants if possible, and pay attention to personal recommendations (and warnings!).

Beware of any lettings agency which tries to make a charge to tenants, eg for providing lists of properties. Reputable agencies do not do this. *Ever*.

Don't rely on informal or verbal agreements, even between friends or family members. Friendships can cool down and if something goes wrong you need the protection of a written tenancy agreement. If you're in any doubt, have your tenancy agreement checked over by a professional (solicitor, housing advisor, CAB specialist) before you sign it.

Be aware of the type of tenancy you are signing up for. Are you a tenant or a licensee? Do you have any security of tenure or any right to appeal against rent increases? Are there any special clauses in your tenancy agreement? If so, can you live with them? What if the agreement specifically prohibits children and you later become pregnant? Is there a mortgage on the property you want to rent? If so, has the owner obtained the necessary permission to let from his bank or building society?

5

Surviving successfully as a tenant is all about planning ahead. This chapter is about how to prepare for the beginning and end of your tenancy; about moving in and moving out.

Moving In

Planning to move into your new home can be quite a tricky process. There are so many imponderables that need to be considered, for example:

- do you wait until you're absolutely sure you've got the house or flat before telling everybody your new address?
- when should you give notice to your present landlord?
- should you allow for an overlap with your last property, or will you take a chance and move in on the day your last tenancy expires?
- does your new home have everything you need, or are there things you need to budget for and buy before you move in?

Keep calm, don't panic and remember: no matter how hard you try to be the perfect organising genius, you're bound to forget something. Everybody does. The trick is to make sure it isn't something vital!

Giving notice

If you're already a tenant, your tenancy agreement will probably lay down the minimum period of notice which you are required to give. In many cases this is one month, sometimes two or even three.

Especially when the notice period is a long one, you really do need to plan ahead, but this can be difficult as landlords and agencies often don't advertise properties until a week or two before they become vacant. So you may find yourself in the position of having to give notice without knowing for certain that you have another property to go to.

Another consideration is whether or not you want an overlap between the start of your new tenancy and the end of your old one. On the negative side, every day or week's overlap will cost you money - and in many cases you may have to end your tenancy on a particular day of the month, which may mean having either no overlap at all or one which is much longer than you want.

On the plus side, an overlap can be a great stress-reliever - if you can afford it. It allows you to move all your stuff out and get settled into your new home, then go back to your old home and attend to any cleaning or repairs before the final inspection and inventory. An unfurnished house is a darned sight easier to clean than a furnished one, and it can be difficult to cope with moving out, moving in and making the old property ship-shape, all in one day.

When you're moving from one end of the country to the other, this can be especially tricky - so if there are two of you, it may be a good idea for one to go ahead to the new house, while the other stays behind to finish the cleaning, check the inventory and hand back the keys.

Setting a date

Once you've given notice and arranged to sign your new agreement and pay the deposit, you can fix a date to move in.

This may or may not be the same day that the tenancy begins. It will depend on a number of factors. For example, your landlord may have agreed to allow you to redecorate before you move in; or you may need to move in urgently because your last property has become uninhabitable (eg through fire or water damage).

When you're fixing the date, it's worth bearing in mind your various work and personal commitments.

Ask yourself:

- can I get time off work?
- can I sign the agreement on a Friday and move in over the weekend?
- do I need to move in on a weekday, so that deliveries can be made to the property or tradesmen can carry out work on it?
- which date will cause least disruption to my work? my family? my pets? (will your kids settle in best at their new school if they join at the beginning of a new term?)
- which date will cause me least expense? (For example, if a removal firm has to keep your furniture in storage, eg over a holiday period, this could prove expensive)

Utilities

Many landlords and agencies will tell the gas, electricity and water companies that you are moving in, and when. On the other hand, they may just leave it to you. Check this well in advance of your moving-in date, or you could end up without a supply!

Also, check whose responsibility it is to take meter readings, and when. Should you 'phone them through to the electricity company on the day you move in? Is there an application form you have to fill in to apply for a gas supply?

If there are gas or electricity meters, is the supply paid for with coins or tokens? If there's a water meter, who's responsible for paying the water bill?

As a tenant, you may find that the utilities regard you with slight suspicion until you've proved that you're a reliable (and solvent) customer. If you're moving into a new area and haven't had an account with the company before, they may ask you to sign up for a monthly payment plan, rather than paying your bills as and when they arrive. If you won't or can't do this, they may insist on payment of a deposit before the supply can be transferred to you.

If this is likely to cause you problems, talk to your landlord and the utility companies before you sign the tenancy agreement. Trained financial advisors at Citizens Advice Bureaux may be able to help with advice on drawing up monthly and weekly budget plans.

The council

Again, landlords will generally inform the council that you are about to move in. If you don't hear from the council within a few weeks of moving in, check that they have been notified.

The council will send you a Council Tax assessment, based on the charge band for your home. They will also advise you on the procedure to apply for help with paying the tax, or any rebate/discount which is owing to you.

If your name doesn't appear on the electoral register, you will lose your voting rights. This can be a big problem for anyone who has to move around a lot (I once moved three times in a year, throwing the entire system into confusion) but do make a nuisance of yourself down the Town Hall, and insist on your rights. If you're given a form to fill in, to be included on the voting register, don't chuck it in the bin. Tenants have a right to a voice, too!

Redirecting your mail

I blanch when I think of the number of times I have applied for mail redirection... and I try not to think about the cost.

Nevertheless, I can't stress too much how important it is to have your mail properly redirected. A friend of mine discovered a couple of years ago that she was on a credit blacklist. Apparently, she had moved house and a later tenant had got hold of one of her electricity bills, which had not been forwarded to her new address. He had used the name and address on the bill to apply for credit in her name...and then defaulted on the payments.

All sorts of important items can go astray if you rely on informal arrangements to redirect your mail, so it makes sense to go along to your local post office and apply for mail redirection. You can apply for a period of three months, six months or a year, and just before the period expires you'll receive a reminder. The service isn't cheap, though. At the time of writing it cost £30 per surname to redirect mail within the UK for one year. (If there are two or more of you, and you have different surnames, each will have to pay £30.)

It's also worth mentioning that the service isn't infallible. I once went back to make a final check on a property I'd vacated a couple of weeks before. Although I'd paid for redirection, I found an envelope containing my new cheque card, sitting happily on the doormat in full view of anyone who cared to look.

My advice is, take out mail redirection if you can possibly afford it; most of the time it works well. But if you can, cover yourself by leaving a forwarding address for the next tenants, plus a note asking them nicely to redirect any items of mail to you. There are bound to be a few items which slipthrough the net.

If you're planning an overlap in your tenancies, it may be worth applying for redirection to start a few days before you actually move: that way, you can see if it's working and do something about it if it isn't.

By the way, the Royal Mail redirection service doesn't cover parcels; but the application form gives a number you can ring to arrange redirection of these.

Change of address cards

These can be printed up very cheaply using the do-it-yourself business-card machines found in railway stations, hypermarkets, shopping malls and the like.

Television

Except in exceptional circumstances, tenants are liable to buy their own television licences. If you have a licence for your last property and it still has some time left to run, you can take it to the post office and have the address changed.

Incidentally, the TV Licensing Centre is a determined creature: I am still receiving TV licence reminders for a property I moved out of over a year ago.

Pets

If you're bringing pets into your new home, it may be a good idea for all concerned to find them alternative accommodation for a few days, until you've settled into your new home.

Reputable kennels, catteries or obliging friends can take a lot of stress out of moving, both for you and your pets. Everyone hates chaos and disruption, and animals are no exception. What's more, there's nothing like a cat for running away and getting locked in someone's shed, or a dog for getting under the removal men's feet.

Choose kennels or catteries well in advance: don't leave it to the last minute, as good ones tend to be booked up quickly, especially during holiday periods.

Removals

If you live close to your new home and have a car (or a friend with a car), it may be feasible to do all the moving yourself, especially if you are going into furnished accommodation and don't have many possessions.

Renting a van is another option which many people choose. It's certainly cheaper than hiring a professional removals firm, and most of the vans on offer can be driven on an ordinary clean car licence. But do bear in mind that moving beds, boxes, cookers etc is a heavy job and you'll probably need help. Friends are often tempted by the promise of a free meal when the job's done!

If you decide to hire a firm, find out whether your employer is prepared to contribute anything to your moving costs. Arrangements don't tend to be as lavish as they used to be, but there are still some generous employers around.

It's advisable to obtain three quotations from removal firms, and compare the prices carefully. If there are wide variations, why? What is one firm offering that another isn't? Don't be afraid to ask questions, and don't hire a firm if you don't feel comfortable about the service they provide.

Insurance is important too. Reputable firms will offer comprehensive insurance against loss, breakages etc - but do read the small print in case you have to make a claim.

On the day

On the day you move into your new home, you will be exhausted, excited, and maybe even a little sad to be leaving your old home. In all the turmoil, there are certain things you need to do:

- Keys: do you have all the keys to the property? Is there a set for each tenant? Do they work properly?
- Meter readings: have these been done, and the readings 'phoned through where necessary?
- Gas, electricity, water, telephone: are all services connected and functioning properly? (And have the installations been checked recently for safety?)
- The inventory: you should have been given two copies of this by your landlord or agency, one to keep and one to be signed and returned. You will probably have seven days in which to check through the inventory and note down anydiscrepancies. You must do this, and do it properly. It is boring and time-consuming, but it could save you money and hassles when you come to the end of the tenancy. Check for:

  Appliances: do they work properly?
  House/flat contents: are they all as described in the inventory? Are they damaged or marked in any way? Is everything you were told would be there, actually there?
  Structure and fabric of the property: is there any damage/disrepair? If you were told that repairs would be carried out, has this been done, and to an acceptable standard?

Don't forget to look under and behind things - it's amazing what can be hidden by artfully-placed items of furniture.

Neighbours...

...everybody needs good neighbours. Unfortunately we don't always get them.

It's funny how being a tenant can lower your status in the eyes of some other people. The key is to change their expectations of you. Some people will never respond, but it's always worth trying. Make a point of introducing yourself to the neighbours; it's good PR, and you never know when you'll need their help.

If you have dogs or cats, it may be a good idea to tell neighbours and make it clear that you're a responsible pet owner. If any problems do arise in the future, you want to feel you can talk them through and sort them out, rather than coming to blows across the garden fence.

Moving Out

Inevitably the day will come when you want, or need, to move on. As with moving in, you need to plan for the event in advance. If you're on a six or twelve-month assured shorthold tenancy, and know that it won't be renewed, you will already have a leaving date more or less fixed in your mind at the start of the tenancy.

Giving notice

As we've already seen, timing is very important here. You need to feel that you're giving yourself enough time to find another place, without committing yourself to a lot of unnecessary expense.

Check your tenancy agreement for the amount of notice which you are required to give (it is often one month, but it does vary). If you are on an assured shorthold tenancy, you are committed to pay the rent until your six months have expired, and you will have to give notice that you intend to leave then.

Remember that once you have given notice, your landlord will be entitled to look for a replacement tenant. This means that people will be coming to see the property, which can be inconvenient if there are a lot of them. You are entitled to insist that they come at times convenient to you, and if need be that they are accompanied by the landlord or his/her representative.

A few months before you want to move, start looking for another place. Agencies may be willing to register you even if they don't yet have anything suitable. But you'll need to keep ringing up (say, once a week), to check the current position - you can't sit back and rely on them ringing you. Also the position can change very rapidly, and if there's something perfect you'll need to be ready to pounce.

If you're moving to another area, you can arrange for local newspapers to be sent to you - this will give you a good idea of prices, the range on offer and names/numbers of local lettings agencies. You could also place a 'wanted' ad if nothing suitable has turned up within a week or two.

Mail redirection

Obtain application forms from your local post office, and make sure that they are submitted at least ten days before you want the redirection to start.

Pets

Book kennels, catteries etc well in advance of your moving date. Make sure that all inoculations are up to date.

Utilities

Your landlord may take care of informing the utilities. It may be a good idea to contact them yourself, to arrange for final bills to be sent promptly. The sooner these are settled, the sooner you will be entitled to repayment of your security deposit.

Meter readings should be taken when you leave - take copies of these for yourself, in case of any dispute.

The check-out inventory

In the days leading up to your departure, you should return everything to the place it was in when you arrived. Also, you should begin checking for any signs of wear and tear, damage, breakages, missing items etc. Incidentally, it helps if you keep a log of minor damage, breakages etc throughout your tenancy. This makes it much easier to remember if it is five or six wine-glasses that you need to replace! You can also keep a note of the dates you informed your landlord of any damage, or repairs which needed carrying out.

Referring to your copy of the inventory, work your way meticulously through the property, checking every item. Ask yourself:

- is everything here that should be here?
- is anything damaged, broken or missing? If so, can it be repaired or replaced? In the case of repairs, are they your responsibility or the landlord's?

- is everything where it should be?
- does anything need cleaning? If so, is it your responsibility to have it cleaned?

You should find your inventory very helpful, provided you went through it carefully when you moved in. Even if you know that the carpet had a hole in it when you moved in, your landlord doesn't have to take your word for it unless you noted it down on the inventory.

When you have left, your landlord (or an inventory clerk) will check the property against your inventory, and deduct money from your deposit to put any deficiencies right. It is well worth spending time (and if necessary a little money) making the property look absolutely brilliant, because this is likely to save you money in the long run.

Never try to conceal damage which you (or your guests) have done. Inventory clerks and landlords have seen every trick in the book, and you simply won't get away with it. In this case, honesty really is the best policy: if you can't repair the damage to a good standard, be upfront and report what has happened.

If you have pets, or are a smoker, your tenancy agreement may specify that you must have carpets and/or curtains cleaned at the end of your tenancy. Obviously this is difficult to do whilst you are still living in the property, so your landlord may be prepared to have the work done and then send you an invoice.

If you are arranging to have work done (eg carpet cleaning), it is a good idea to ask your landlord or agency for the names of recommended firms - if there are any disputes as to the quality of the work, you can point out that the firm was recommended by your landlord. Don't do this type of work yourself without your landlord's approval: s/he may insist on it being done professionally.

Moving on

Once you are satisfied that the house is clean, tidy and in good order, you can hand back the keys and walk away. Within a few weeks you should have received your deposit (less any deductions). If not, it is time to ask serious questions.

If there are disputes about any deductions made, refer to your inventory and the log which you have kept: can you prove that you were not responsible for the damage? Could anyone else have been responsible? If you took photographs of the property when you moved in, these may provide valuable evidence which will make the landlord back down. On occasion landlords will 'try it on' - they may feel they can intimidate you into paying to have a room redecorated, or a carpet replaced, rather than paying for it themselves.

Summing up

Planning is an important part of successful moving. With thought and organisation, you can ensure that your tenancy begins and ends without too many hitches.

Remember:

- think carefully about the right moving date for you, before you give notice to your landlord
- be aware of your obligations under the tenancy agreement
- notify gas, electricity, water and telephone companies in advance of arrival and departure
- have your mail redirected
- think about putting pets into kennels until you've settled in
- work through the check-in inventory meticulously, and note down every discrepancy: a failure to do so could cost you your deposit
- work through the check-out inventory carefully, and make sure that any damage, loss or breakage has been made good

- have carpets and curtains cleaned if this is required by your agreement
- don't conceal damage: you're very unlikely to get away with it
- take time to put the property into excellent order before you leave

6

You're in your new home now, but that's not the end of it. It's time to take careful stock of where you stand.

Surviving as a tenant isn't just about knowing your rights and paying your rent on time; it's also about being a *good* tenant, about knowing and carrying out your obligations.

The tenancy agreement (which we looked at in detail in Chapter 4: Red Tape) is in effect a set of undertakings made by you and your landlord, promising to behave in a certain way. If either of you breach the undertakings you have made, you could render the tenancy agreement void.

A civilised arrangement?

Many of the problems associated with being a tenant come from the mistaken belief that landlords and tenants have completely opposite interests. According to popular belief, a landlord's idea of the perfect tenant is someone who pays the rent two weeks early, never complains about anything, does all the repairs himself and is hardly ever around.

A tenant's idea of the perfect landlord might be someone who let him live rent-free in a palace, paid all the bills and installed a jacuzzi free of charge. Let's be realistic about this. It's true that landlords let property primarily to make money, and there will always be some tenants who want something for nothing. But a good relationship between landlord and tenant can be beneficial to everyone.

If you have a good landlord, you will probably feel a sense of obligation and responsibility - and you will certainly feel more inclined to treat his or her property with respect. Good landlords realise that good tenants protect, maintain and care for their property. What's more, landlords are very much aware which of their tenants are good, and which are bad. It tends to be the good ones who have their tenancies renewed, and obtain the kind of references which make it easy to obtain tenancies elsewhere.

What you should ask for from your landlord

There are a number of features which it is reasonable for you to expect from your tenancy (as opposed to a licence) :

- the right to exclusive use of a property, or a specific part of it
- the right to occupy the property for the length of time set out in your tenancy agreement
- accommodation and facilities as set out in the agreement
- a home fit for habitation
- a safe environment
- freedom from harassment
- notice (as specified in the agreement) if your landlord wishes to bring the tenancy to an end and/or begin possession proceedings
- proper notification and discussion of any problems or grievances

What your landlord should ask from you

Tenancy is a two-way process, so it is only fair that your landlord also obtains some benefits from you:

- payment of your rent in full and on time
- good ('tenantlike') behaviour, which doesn't damage the property or cause nuisance to other people
- reasonable access to the property when needed, to carry out inspections or repairs
- notice (as specified in the agreement) if you wish to end the tenancy
- proper notification and discussion of any problems or grievances

It should be stressed that not all of the above are your automatic right in law; but they are points that indicate the quality of the landlord/tenant relationship.

That's *your* job!

Some of the biggest problems between landlords and tenants arise because of disputes over who is responsible for what. It's a bit late to sort this out when a burst water-pipe is flooding your living-room, so try to find out about your rights and obligations early on in your tenancy.

Repairs and maintenance

The law affecting the responsibility for repairing and maintaining rented property is a hotch-potch of Acts of Parliament, common law (made by judges) and the terms of your tenancy agreement.

Your tenancy agreement

Before doing anything else, take a good hard look at your tenancy agreement. Does it set out in detail who is responsible for carrying out repairs? It may state that you, the tenant, are liable for minor procedures such as changing light-bulbs and fuses - but what about the reponsibility for unblocking the drains and guttering, or mending the gas boiler? It's fairly common for tenants to be made liable for internal decorations, although these may not be mentioned in the tenancy agreement at all.

In rare instances, the landlord may state in the agreement that he will carry out all repairs; if this is the case, this undertaking can be enforced in law. However, it is rare, and only covers repairs, not improvements.

Even if the agreement states that you are responsible for all the repairs, this may not be enforceable in law; it depends on your type of tenancy and the nature of the repairs. So take legal advice before despairing.

What the law says

Under common law, your landlord has an obligation to ensure that furnished lettings are fit for human habitation, although he can't actually be forced to make the property habitable. Your duty under common law is to use the property in a 'tenantlike' manner. This means looking after it, and doing small jobs like mending fuses and having the chimney swept.

The *Landlord and Tenant Act 1985* gives a list of the landlord's obligations, which are:

- to keep the structure and exterior of the property in repair. This includes guttering, drains and external pipes
- to keep in repair and good working order installations for the supply of water, gas, electricity and sanitation. This includes basins, baths, sinks and lavatories
- to keep in repair and proper working order installations for room and water heating

If the rent payable is very low (£80 pa or less in London, £52 or less elsewhere), the landlord must also ensure that the house is fit for habitation and remains so throughout the whole of the tenancy. Usually, the tenancy agreement will allow your landlord access to the property for inspections and to carry out repairs, though he should give you reasonable notice unless it's an emergency.

Other laws may also be relevant to your situation. *The Environmental Protection Act 1990* deals mainly with public health issues, and preventing 'statutory nuisance'. But if your property is 'in such a state as to be prejudicial to health or a nuisance', you may be able to get help through your local Environmental Health Officer. Other relevant legislation includes the *Housing Act 1985* (which deals with houses unfit for human habitation, and fit houses in need of repair).

Public sector tenancies

Since 1 January 1986, these have been covered by the *Secure Tenancies (Right to Repair Scheme) Regulations 1985*.

Tenants must serve notice to their landlord, setting out the work that needs to be done, why it should be done and the materials which need to be used. The landlord must reply within 21 days, agreeing to the claim or refusing it. The regulations are quite complicated, and there are instances where the landlord is within his rights to refuse.

Safety regulations

Under recent gas safety regulations, your landlord is obliged to have all gas appliances checked over at least once a year, by a CORGI approved engineer.

He must also keep a record of all these inspections, and any maintenance carried out, and make it available for you to consult.

Although gas safety is your landlord's obligation, it is better to be safe than sorry. You owe it to yourself to buy carbon monoxide detectors if you can afford them. If not, ask your landlord if these can be installed, along with smoke detectors to improve fire safety.

In most cases, soft furnishings and mattresses must comply with the *Furniture (Fire) (Safety) Regulations 1988*, which set out a number of flammability tests.

If you live in a block of flats, hostel or bedsit, check that any relevant fire regulations are being observed.

Getting repairs carried out

It is your job to notify your landlord if something needs repairing, and it's in your interests to do it as soon as you notice that something is wrong. If you don't do this, and you are later injured because the repairs weren't carried out, your landlord may not be liable for the injuries you have suffered and you won't have any means of redress.

If there is any possibility of dispute, it is advisable to notify your landlord in writing about repairs which need to be done, and keep a copy for future reference.

Gardens

If the property has a garden, you will probably be expected to keep it in good order; if so, tools should be provided for your use - and the garden should be in a reasonable condition to start off with. If it is a garden shared with other tenants (eg the garden to a house converted into several flats) you may share the responsibility for keeping it tidy.

Occasionally, the landlord will insist on the use of a professional gardening service, the cost of which will be included in your rent. This is quite common where the landlord is (say) living abroad, is letting out his home through an agency and is concerned to make sure that the property doesn't lose any of its value by being allowed to fall into disrepair. If you are a very keen gardener and desperately want to do the gardening yourself, you will need to negotiate.

If the gardens are in very bad condition - I once nearly rented a house whose garden was an overgrown mess of old bedsteads and sump-oil - it is best to insist that they are properly cleared before you move in. Don't be tempted to accept vague promises, either: have it written into your agreement.

Summing up

Utilities

Your landlord is obliged to keep all installations in repair and good working order.

Safety

If you have notified your landlord that a repair needs to be carried out, and you are later injured because it hasn't been, your landlord might be liable in some degree for your injuries.

Under gas safety regulations, gas installations and appliances must be checked at least annually, and records kept for inspection by tenants.

Soft furnishings must comply with recent flammability regulations. If you are bringing your own furniture to a rented property, does it comply with the 1988 regulations? If not, can it be replaced?

Be aware of your own responsibility, and take any additional measures you can to improve your safety, eg installing smoke alarms. Your landlord may be willing to install these, if not to protect you then to protect his property.

Internal decoration

This may well be your responsibility, though it depends on what is laid down in the tenancy agreement and what you and your landlord decide between yourselves. It's unwise to carry out any major redecoration without first obtaining your landlord's approval.

Gardens

These may be your responsibility, or a responsibility shared with other tenants. Alternatively, you may be asked to contribute to the cost of having them professionally maintained.

Improvements

Generally speaking, your landlord is only responsible for repairs, not for improvements, unless these are specifically mentioned in your tenancy agreement. For example, he might be liable to repair existing broken guttering, but not to install guttering if the house didn't have any already.

Insurance

Your landlord is responsible for insuring the property and any contents which belong to him. You must not behave in a way which would infringe the insurance company's requirements, or cause the premium to be raised. It is in your interests to take out insurance to cover your own belongings.

Talking things over

A politician once commented that 'jaw, jaw is better than war, war', and talking to your landlord is certainly preferable to firing off angry letters.

One way to prevent disputes is to sit down with your landlord and draw up a list of who is going to be responsible for what - but remember that the law may overrule whatever you have decided, even if you both agree.

Of course, even well thought-out agreements can throw up problems, and even the best tenants can sometimes find themselves in dispute with their landlords. In Chapter 8 (Troubleshooting), we take a look at what you can do to get yourself out of some sticky situations.

7

So far, we've looked at what it's like to be a tenant, and ways of making your life a little easier. We tend to think that there is no connection between being a tenant and being a homeowner, but this isn't always the case. This chapter is about ways of buying your rented home.

The public sector

If you are a local authority tenant, you will most probably already know about the Right to Buy scheme.

This was introduced back in 1980, and has proved very popular with tenants. If you live in a house, you have the right to buy the freehold in it; if you're a flat-dweller, you can't buy the freehold, but you can acquire a 125-year lease.

The residence qualification

In order to qualify for the scheme, you (or your partner) must have been resident in public sector accommodation for at least two years, although not necessarily in the same house or flat. So if you've only just moved in, or are about to acquire your first council flat, you will have to wait to acquire the right to buy.

How is the price determined?

In theory, the price you pay for your property is the price you would pay on the open market; but in practice this isn't the case, because of the generous discounts offered to tenants. The amount of discount you get depends on how long you've been in public sector accommodation, and you will also get a bigger discount for a flat than on a house (flats are harder to sell).

The minimum discount you will get on the price of your house is 32% of its market value, plus another 1% for every complete year of residence. The maximum discount you can get is 60%. For a flat, you will get a minimum discount of 44% plus another 2% for every complete year of residence. The maximum discount you can get is 70%. The maximum value of the discount you can get on any purchase is £50,000. If you think the local authority has set the price of your property too high, you have three months to appeal to the District Valuer. His decision is final.

What if you want to sell?

The snag is that if you want to sell your property within three years of buying it, you will have to repay some or all of the discount you have been given. This is designed to stop people making a 'fast buck' out of buying at a low price and selling at a huge profit.

That being said, if you want to give your house to someone, you can do this at any time without penalty, and if you die your heirs won't have to pay back the discount. Once you've owned the property for three years, you can sell it without having to repay any of the discount.

Rent-to-mortgage

This is a variation of the right-to-buy scheme, which has been introduced to help less well-off tenants to buy their homes without it costing them any more in mortgage payments than they're already paying in rent.

In effect, the landlord makes an 'interest-free loan' to the tenant, to whom the freehold of the house is transferred. This 'loan' has to be paid back only if the house is sold, or if the tenant dies.

So is it worth buying?

There's no doubt that the right-to-buy scheme has proved extremely popular with council tenants: to date, over a million have taken advantage of the scheme.

Pros

- if you're paying a mortgage on your house rather than rent, you're contributing towards a valuable asset which will one day be yours
- you will be offered a generous discount on the open market value of your property
- you will eventually have something which you can sell, or leave to your family in your will
- once you are an owner rather than a tenant, you can make changes to the property without having to obtain permission from the council (although you may need to obtain planning permission for major changes)

Cons

- if you need to sell within three years, you will have to pay back some of the discount you have received
- once you own your property, you will be responsible for the cost of repairs etc: owning can work out more expensive than renting
- some people have had difficulty in keeping up with the mortgage payments (which may vary dramatically, according to changes in the bank rate). If you fall behind with payments, you could have your home repossessed. As a secure tenant, you enjoy considerable security of tenure

- some properties, especially flats, can be difficult to sell on. Before you decide whether or not to buy, it's worth taking a good look at the property and its location, and perhaps talking to an estate agent about the likely saleability of the property
- the prices of ex-council properties may be appreciably lower than the prices of very similar, privately-built properties

In the end, of course, it comes down to a purely personal decision. Most of us have a hankering to own our own homes. But it's important to look carefully at your personal circumstances before making a choice.

Leasehold property

The tenants of properties with long leases now have rights which may enable them to buy their freehold (in the case of houses) or an extended lease (in the case of flats).

Houses

In some parts of the country, leasehold houses are quite common. These are houses which effectively belong to the tenant, but which are built on land belonging to a landlord. Under the *Leasehold Reform Act 1967* (which was amended in 1993), the tenants of houses with long leases at a low ground rent have the right to 'enfranchisement': that is, the right to buy the freehold. Alternatively, they can choose to extend their lease for another 50 years.

Who can buy?

The rules are quite complicated. In order to qualify, you must fulfil certain conditions:

- you must be an 'individual' (eg as opposed to a company)
- you must have the lease of a house
- you must have occupied the house as your only or main home for the last three years, or for three out of the last ten years

- you must have a long lease (originally granted for more than 21 years, although you don't have to be the original tenant)
- the ground rent must be low
- in some cases, the house must fall within specified rateable value limits

Should you buy the freehold?

There are two big advantages to buying the freehold of your house:

- it will increase the value of the property
- in the long term, when you take ground rent into consideration, it will actually cost more to buy an extended lease than to buy the freehold

How is the price determined?

If you and your landlord can't agree a price, an expert valuer should be called in. The price is likely to be fixed somewhere between 10 and 20 times the ground rent, plus the cost of your own and your landlord's legal and surveying fees.

If you're not happy with the price, you can appeal to a leasehold valuation tribunal.

What to do next

When you've decided what you want to do, you must serve a 'desire notice' on your landlord, telling him that you want to buy the freehold (or an extended lease). You can get a printed form for this from any legal stationer.

Your landlord must reply to the notice within two months, either agreeing or objecting to your claim.

Flats

Usually, when you buy a flat you are buying a long lease rather than the freehold. The lengths of leases vary, but if your flat has a lease which has only 50 years or less left to run, you may find it very difficult to sell. Mortgage lenders are also often reluctant to lend on leases of 60 years or less.

Under the *Leasehold Reform, Housing and Urban Development Act 1993*, flat owners have the right to band together and jointly buy the freehold to their block of flats. Alternatively, you have the right to buy an extended lease of your flat, adding an extra 90 years to your existing lease.

Your landlord

Either the freehold or a longer lease can be bought without your landlord's consent, except in a few limited cases.

Your landlord can dispute your right to buy the freehold or a new lease only if he can show that the qualifying conditions haven't been met, or (in certain rare cases) if he intends to redevelop the block and most of the long leases are due to terminate within 5 years.

Buying the freehold

Flat owners can collectively buy the freehold in their block of flats. They have to buy the freehold in the whole block - you can't just buy the freehold to the flat you live in. This means that there has to be a lot of co-operation between flat owners in the block.

Once the freehold has been bought, the flat owners can take over management of the block and grant themselves new long leases. Managing the block yourselves eliminates the problem of landlords who don't carry out maintenance, or overcharge tenants for it.

How do you qualify?

Both residence and building qualifications have to be satisfied.

According to the residence qualification, the flat-owner must be the tenant of a flat on a long lease and at a low rent. He must have occupied the flat as his only or main home for the last 12 months or for 3 out of the last 10 years.

To buy the freehold, at least two-thirds of qualifying tenants must take part and at least half of these must satisfy the residence qualification.

According to the building qualification, the building in which the flats are situated must satisfy the Act's rather involved definition of 'premises'.

How is the price determined?

You will have to pay the open-market price for the freehold, plus possible compensation to the landlord if buying the freehold reduces the value of any other property in the area which belongs to him. You may also have to pay a share of other costs.

What to do

The first thing to do is find out how many of the other flat owners are interested in buying the freehold of the block. If enough are interested, and qualify for the scheme, you can then ask a qualified valuer to give you some idea of the price you'll be asked to pay. Now is the time to get professional advice.

Once you have served notice on the freeholder (your landlord), you will have to pay the landlord's costs if you decide to withdraw from the purchase.

If there are four flat-owners or fewer, you can buy the freehold jointly and hold it on trust for yourselves. If there are more than four, you will probably have to set up a limited company to buy the freehold on your behalf. You will then all become shareholders.

Buying a longer lease

Rather than go through the process of jointly purchasing the freehold, many people prefer simply to buy an extended lease for their own flat. This makes it easier to sell and doesn't involve you in the many hassles of running a block of flats. Also, you can buy an extended lease on your own flat even if the other flat owners don't want to have anything to do with the scheme.

How do you qualify?

To buy an extended lease, you must have occupied the flat as your own or principal home for the last 3 years or for 3 out of the last 10 years.

Other types of tenancy: buying your home

Owners sometimes turn to letting when they can't quite decide what they want to do with their property - for example, if your landlord is working abroad and isn't sure if and when he's coming back, or if he wants to sell at some point in the future, but the housing market is flat.

If you know that your landlord is thinking of selling, you like where you're living and you think you can afford to buy, there's absolutely nothing to stop you making an offer. You may get a particularly good deal, if your landlord is in a hurry to sell and is attracted by the idea of a ready-made buyer. But before you make an offer, check out the local market and get the advice of a qualified valuer.

Summing up

Tenancy can sometimes act as a lead-in to home ownership. If you're a public sector tenant, the discounts offered on the open market price can be a big incentive to buy. It can also be an attractive proposition to buy the freehold of a leasehold property, as this can increase its value and make it much more attractive to potential buyers.

But home-ownership isn't without its problems. Some right-to-buy purchasers have had their homes repossessed because they couldn't keep up the mortgage payments. Some buyers of council flats have discovered that they are extremely difficult to sell.

Joining with other flat-owners to purchase the freehold of the block of flats you live in may solve the problem of paying over the odds for maintenance, but it can bring its own complications. It may be preferable simply to buy an extended lease of your flat.

Before making a decision, ask yourself a few questions:

- buying may be an attractive option, but is it the right one for you?
- can you afford the mortgage payments and other outgoings which home-ownership brings?
- if you're a public sector tenant, might you need to re-sell the property within three years?
- will buying your home provide you with something you really want and need?
- if you're in a flat, do you really want to buy the freehold of the whole block, or just an extended lease?

8

It's a great flat, you love the area, you can afford the rent, the landlord is terrific, the next-door neighbour adores your pet piranha fish... then, all of a sudden, something goes horribly wrong.

Every tenant has them; those problems that strike out of the blue and send you into a panic, or the slow-burning ones that begin as distant niggles at the back of your mind and turn gradually into high-octane rows. In this chapter, we're going to look at some of the problems you may encounter, and at some of the things you can do to get through them.

What if...

...Your repairs aren't done?

In Chapter 6 (Rights and obligations) we looked at the promises which landlord and tenant make, and the responsibilities which they accept. One of your landlord's obligations is to carry out necessary repairs to the property he lets out (according to the terms of your tenancy agreement). If you have notified him about the repairs, provided they are his responsibility he is obliged to carry them out, even if he can't afford to.

What can you do?

So what do you do if your landlord fails or refuses to keep his side of the bargain? There are several avenues you can consider:

- the legal option: sue your landlord and get a court order which will force him to do the repairs
- the halfway house: pay to have the repairs done yourself, then claim for damages against your landlord. You could also claim for the cost of accommodation during the repairs, if your home was unfit to live in
- the self-help route: give your landlord notice that the repairs need to be done, and allow a suitable amount of time for him to do them. Most of the time, self-help is the best and simplest option and all you need to do is proceed slowly and gently - the courts really are the last resort, and sueing your landlord is hardly going to improve relations between you

The first thing to do is to make absolutely sure that the repairs really are your landlord's liability, and not yours. If there is any doubt at all, get proper legal advice before you do anything. In particular, don't withhold rent as a protest: you could make yourself liable to eviction on the grounds of rent arrears.

If your landlord is dragging his feet, and you are certain that he is responsible for the repairs, you could think about having the work done yourself and then deducting the cost from future rent. Talk to your local Housing Advice Centre or CAB about whether this is an advisable thing to do. If you do decide to try it, you should:

- give your landlord notice that the repairs need to be done
- obtain estimates for the work (at least three), and send the landlord copies
- tell the landlord if he doesn't do the work by a certain date (give him a reasonable amount of time) you will arrange for the work to be done and deduct the cost from future rent

NB - safety first!

If you smell gas, or believe that there is a serious safety hazard in your home, don't hesistate: ring the emergency number in Yellow Pages, get out and then contact your landlord. Your life is too precious to take chances with.

Local authority help

Legislation may also help you in certain circumstances. For example, under Sections 79-82 of the *Environmental Protection Act 1990*, a tenant can ask the local authority to take action if the property could be said to be 'in such a state as to be prejudicial to health or a nuisance'. An environmentalhealth officer will inspect the building and decide if there are grounds to apply for an 'abatement notice'.

The types of 'nuisance' which might be covered include dangerous gas and electrical appliances/installations, crumbling plaster, rising damp and condensation. If a property is considered 'unfit for human habitation' under the *Housing Act 1985*, the local authority can take action ranging from a 'repair notice' to a demolition or clearance order. If theproperty is 'fit but in need of repair', the local authority can serve a repair notice on the landlord, forcing him to have the work done.

...Your landlord wants to put the rent up?

As we saw in Chapter 2 (Are you a tenant?) the amount of control you have over the amount of rent you have to pay depends to a large extent on the type of tenancy you have. Assured tenancies offer you little control over the amount of rent you have to pay. Assured shortholds give you some protection against 'excessive' rents, which means that you can appeal to a rent assessment committee - although the rent will only be reduced if it's seen to be 'significantly higher' than the market level.

It's worth bearing in mind that your landlord may not be able to increase the rent unless he follows a set procedure. Your housing advice centre or CAB will advise on this. Your local social security office can provide information on benefits which may be available to help you pay any legitimate rent increase.

If your tenancy was granted before 15 January 1989 and comes under the *Rent Act 1977*, your tenancy is subject to the 'fair rent' system. The amount of rent payable is assessed by a local rent officer, and this tends to keep rents lower than the open market rate. You can apply for an assessment at any time, and the amount decided can't be changed for two years.

...You find yourself in financial problems?

It's distressing enough to lose your job, without having to worry about whether or not you're going to lose your home as well.

Unlike home owners, tenants don't have redundancy protection insurance to cushion them against loss of earnings. There are lots of other possible causes of a temporary or permanent drop in income: death of a partner, breakup of a relationship, debt, failure of a business, illness, birth of a child etc. And no matter how little you have coming into the house, you still have to find the money for the rent each week or month.

There are a number of things you can do if you find yourself getting into deep financial water:

- talk to your bank or building society: can they help you to budget, or offer loan arrangements to tide you over a short period of difficulty?
- see a financial advisor at your CAB, and try to work out a budget. Can you afford to pay the rent, or is it going to be impossible?
- talk to a housing advisor about your options
- talk to your local social security office about benefits which may be available to help you (these are discussed more fully at the end of this book)
- talk to your landlord/agency *before* you default on your rent. It may be possible to work something out. In some cases, a landlord will release you early from an assured shorthold tenancy if you need to move to a cheaper property, particularly if someone else can be found to take over your tenancy
- in some cases your landlord may give you permission to take in a lodger or joint tenant, to share the rent and ease your financial situation: but you *mustn't* do this without your landlord's approval, particularly if it is prohibited by your tenancy agreement

....You have problems with the neighbours?

It can be an uphill struggle to be regarded on equal terms with a terrace-full of homeowners, and if there are any prejudices around, you can be sure they will stick like flying mud to any tenants who happen to be in the vicinity.

I have experienced a variety of bizarre behaviour from neighbours, from the woman who regarded my garden as her own (and climbed into it at dead of night to plant a rhododendron), to the neighbours who conspired to have all the trees in the street pruned *except* the one outside my house, leaving one tree fifteen feet taller than all the rest. My cats have had bricks, buckets, water, mud and a lot worse thrown at them. Complete strangers have parked their cars in my driveway. A flat-dwelling friend of mine even endured a neighbour who insisted that she must cover all her walls with aluminium foil, to 'protect her from the cosmic rays'. It's a funny old world, but no funnier than the people who live in it.

Frankly there's not a lot you can do about people's attitudes, other than behave impeccably and make it clear that you have just as much right to be where you are as they do. If anyone does something which damages the property you're living in, that's a different matter and should be referred to the landlord and/or police, whichever seems more appropriate. If neighbours spread malicious rumours about you in an attempt to force you out, this is also a matter for the authorities.

...Your landlord harrasses you?

Harassment, violence and unlawful eviction are very real problems. Some unscrupulous landlords will do practically anything rather than resort to the courts, perhaps because possession proceedings don't always produce the desired effect and threats are a much cheaper way to force a tenant out onto the street.

Harassment can take many forms, but can include such things as threats, acts of violence, removing doors and windows, or cutting off the water, gas and electricity.

If you are being harassed or threatened by your landlord, you must begin by taking advice. This area of the law is complex and you need a knowledgeable hand to guide you. Also - and most importantly of all - you should never take risks with your own safety.

Basically, there are two ways in which you can fight unlawful eviction: civil action and criminal proceedings. The courts can order damages in compensation for any loss suffered, or an injunction which prevents the landlord from threatening you and allows you to return to your home.

Criminal proceedings

There are two main laws affecting unlawful eviction: the *Protection from Eviction Act 1977* and the *Criminal Law Act 1977*.

Under the Protection from Eviction Act it's an offence to evict you without a court order, unless your landlord has reason to believe that you no longer live in the property. Your landlord can be imprisoned or fined for harassment and unlawful eviction, and you can be awarded compensation. The local authority will usually use this Act against a landlord.

The police can bring proceedings against landlords under the *Criminal Law Act*. This states that no-one 'without lawful authority' must use, or threaten to use, violence to enter premises if there is someone on the premises who opposes the entry.

Magistrates can order compensation for any loss, damage or personal injury resulting from an offence, and this is easy and cheap for the tenant. But the sums awarded tend to be relatively low, and if you do receive this, it will be deducted from any damages you later receive as a result of a civil action.

Civil proceedings

These are necessary to restrain the landlord or regain possession of the property. The county court can order damages and injunctions, quickly if necessary. The landlord can defend the action if he can show he had cause to believe you were no longer living on the premises, or that he had reasonable grounds for his conduct.

The amount of any damages awarded will vary, according to your own behaviour and that of your landlord. The court can order that you are allowed to return to the property.

Bringing a court action

If you're eligible for legal aid, it's best to instruct a solicitor - it's important to follow the correct procedures. CABs, housing advice centres and law centres are very helpful in giving advice on how to fill in the necessary forms etc. You can obtain the forms at the local office of the county court.

These forms will need to be filled in carefully, and you will need the following information:

- address and full details of the property
- a copy of your tenancy agreement/rent book (if you have access to them)
- full details of the alleged harassment or eviction
- names and addresses of any witnesses
- landlord's full name and address
- details of anyone else involved in the alleged harassment or eviction

Emergency proceedings

In an emergency, for example if you have just been thrown out onto the street, the court can hear what is called an 'ex parte' application, instead of following the usual process of hearing both sides of the argument. Any decision made is only valid until another hearing can be held.

Normally notice of proceedings should be served on the landlord at least two days before the hearing.

Enforcing the order

Sometimes a court order may include a 'penal notice'. This means that if your landlord fails to comply with the terms of the order, you can apply to have him sent to prison. The county court can order a prison term of up to two years, but it can also suspend a committal order and/or order the landlord to pay a fine.

Summing up

Problems can arise between landlord and tenant, often as a result of poorly drawn-up tenancy agreements, or misunderstandings. Better communication can often highlight solutions to these problems, but from time to time you may need to take action to assert your rights.

Remember:

- it pays to know your rights; be absolutely sure that you understand the terms of your tenancy
- never take legal action or withhold rent without taking proper professional advice and knowing exactly where you stand
- keep a record of all contact you have with your landlord, eg requests for repairs to be carried out

In this chapter, we've looked at a range of problems including the threat of unlawful eviction. Next, we will take a look at what you can do if your landlord wants you to leave, and applies to court for a possession order.

9

Perhaps the biggest fear for every tenant is the fear of losing your home. Landlords often underestimate this fear, and some seem to think that tenants see their rented properties as no more than a place to sleep. You may not own your home, but it is still your home; and being told that you must leave it can be very traumatic.

When your tenancy expires, you will normally be expected to leave the property you have been renting. There may be other circumstances in which your landlord wants you to leave - for example if he is coming back from abroad and wants to resume living in his home, or if you haven't been paying the rent on time.

However, as we saw in Chapter 8, if you're a tenant your landlord can't simply tell you to get out, with no notice or compensation. There are proper procedures which must be followed in order to remove a tenant and regain possession of a rented property.

Possession proceedings

The precise procedures which have to be followed vary between the different types of tenancy, and it's important that you take advice about the implications for your individual case. But in this section we'll take a general look at the steps which your landlord will need to go through if he wants to gain a possession order against you.

For most types of tenancy, your landlord will need to obtain a court order for possession if you refuse to leave his property. This means a complex and sometimes lengthy haggle in the courts. A court order isn't necessary in the case of licences and some excluded tenancies (eg holiday lets, residential hostels), as long as your landlord doesn't use or threaten violence towards you. However, your landlord may choose to get a court order anyway if he thinks the situation between you might turn to violence.

Grounds for possession

Getting a court order is dependent on your landlord proving that he has a specified *ground for possession* (either 'mandatory' or 'discretionary'), as defined in law. He must state the ground s/he intends to prove when he makes his application for possession. In the case of mandatory grounds, the court must order possession if they are proved; it has more leeway if only a discretionary ground can be proved. The specific grounds will vary according to the legislation which governs your type of tenancy.

Mandatory grounds include such situations as:

- the owner of your property wishing to move back and live in it as his main home
- the end of a winter let (ie holiday accommodation which is required for the summer season)
- demolition or reconstruction
- repossession by the building society, in order to sell the property
- substantial rent arrears (usually several months' worth)

Discretionary grounds can include:

- rent arrears
- persistent delay in paying rent
- damage to the property or its contents
- 'nuisance' (eg playing loud music, or being convicted of using the property for illegal or immoral purposes)

The termination notice

In order to initiate the process, your landlord must begin by serving a termination notice on you. This notice must take the precise form prescribed by law for your type of tenancy, or else it may be declared invalid.

If you are an assured shorthold tenant, the notice must be served at least two months before your landlord requires possession of the property. In practice, the notice (known as a Section 21 notice) is usually served on you at the beginning of the tenancy, before you sign the agreement. This means that if you don't move out at the end of the agreed fixed term (say, six months), your landlord can start possession proceedings straight away.

The notice period will vary between types of tenancy. In the case of 'occupiers without security of tenure', it is vaguely defined under common law as 'reasonable notice'; so it makes sense to have a notice period specified in a written tenancy agreement.

If you have not left the property by the time the termination notice expires, your landlord will have to begin possession proceedings against you in the county court.

The accelerated possession procedure

This was brought in in November 1993, as a faster alternative to a court hearing. It offers the landlord immediate possession in certain specific circumstances, but does not allow him to claim rent arrears: in order to do this, he must go through the courts in the normal way.

The accelerated possession procedure is only an option if:

- the landlord can prove a mandatory ground for possession
- the tenancy is either assured or an assured shorthold, and a number of other conditions are also satisfied

Your landlord must submit an application for possession, together with a sworn affidavit, and copies of the tenancy agreement and the notices which have been served on you. The court will then serve these papers on you, and you will have 14 days to reply on a printed form.

If you don't reply, your landlord can apply for a possession order. Assuming the court is satisfied, it will make an order for possession and both you and your landlord will be notified. If not, a hearing date will be fixed and you and your landlord will both be asked to come to court.

If an order is made against you, you will normally have to leave your home within 14 days, unless you can prove 'exceptional hardship', when the period may be extended up to a maximum of 42 days.

What happens in ordinary possession hearings?

If the accelerated possession procedure isn't an option, your landlord will need to follow the ordinary possession procedure. He must send the court a summons for possession of the property (with a copy for each tenant), plus details of his claim (with copies), and the court fee. He must set out the grounds under which he's claiming possession, and give details of any rent arrears, your financial circumstances, and any measures which have been taken to recover rent arrears.

The court will usually send the papers to you by first class post. At the same time your landlord will receive a notice of issue, and a date for the court hearing. Technically, you have 14 days to reply on a printed form (supplied with the summons), but in practice you can reply up to the hearing date or even turn up at the hearing to give evidence against your landlord's claim.

The hearing

The hearing will normally be held at a district judge's court, and your landlord will attend to give evidence. You can also attend the hearing and give evidence against the claim.

The court's decision

The court will decide whether or not your landlord has a valid claim for possession. If it feels the claim has not been proved, it can dismiss the application, or order an adjournment to a later date.

If your landlord proves a *mandatory* ground for possession, the court will issue an *absolute order*. This means that you must leave the property on a specified date. If a *discretionary* ground is proved, a *suspended order* may be issued. This is still an order for possession, but it is suspended as long as certain conditions are fulfilled, eg the payment of rent arrears. If you fail to carry out the terms of the order, your landlord can apply to the court for the order to be made absolute.

If your landlord is relying on a discretionary ground, and you haven't committed a serious breach of your tenancy agreement, the court may decide on an adjournment rather than a possession order. This adjournment may be to a specified date, or indefinitely, and will lay down certain conditions which must be fulfilled, eg payment of rent arrears. If these conditions are breached, your landlord could apply for a suspended or absolute order.

If your landlord fails to prove his claim, the court may *dismiss* the proceedings. It may also do this if he failed to follow the correct procedure.

Costs

If possession proceedings are dismissed, you can apply for costs against your landlord. The awarding of costs is at the court's discretion. If your landlord wins a possession order against you, you may have to pay some or all of his costs.

You may have made a *counterclaim* against your landlord (eg if he has failed to carry out repairs). If this succeeds, you may receive damages.

How is a possession order enforced?

If the court makes an absolute order against you, and you haven't left the property by the date set out in the order, your landlord can apply for a *warrant of possession*. If this is awarded, the court bailiff will send you an eviction notice, informing you when the order will be carried out.

You can apply to the court for the warrant to be deferred, but this will only be done if you can show exceptional circumstances.

Fighting your corner

If your landlord starts possession proceedings against you, it's easy to lose your nerve and feel that everything is out of your control. Don't panic! It's important that you keep a cool head, and realise that your landlord's application will not necessarily succeed. The law gives you the right of reply, and if there is a court hearing you can attend to give evidence in your favour.

It takes time to obtain a court order, and grounds for possession must be proved. Even if your landlord does prove his case and wins a court order, if the grounds proved are discretionary it may be suspended and you may be able to stay on in your home. Even if an absolute order is awarded, the court may be able to exercise some discretion on when it is carried out.

Looking at the situation from the other side, it's always possible that you may be able to file a counterclaim against your landlord. For example, he may be claiming rent arrears against you, but you may have withheld rent to cover the cost of repairs which he has failed to carry out.

Getting legal advice

If at all possible, you should obtain some kind of professional help if you intend to defend possession proceedings. A law centre, CAB or housing advice centre is a very useful first stop, for sound legal and practical advice. They can also advise you on what to do if a court order is made against you and you are faced with losing your home.

Not everyone can afford to pay for a solicitor, but you may qualify for Legal Aid. A solicitor can tell you if you are eligible for advice under the 'green form' scheme: if you are on Income Support and don't have much in the way of savings, you will almost certainly qualify. The green form scheme allows a solicitor to give you advice and assistance, but not to act on your behalf in legal proceedings, or represent you at a court hearing.

If you can obtain a civil legal aid certificate, this will entitle you to have a solicitor to represent you in court. The application form will be filled in for you by the solicitor. It goes to the Legal Aid Board, which has to decide whether you qualify on the basis of income, and whether it makes sense for you to defend a possession action or make a counterclaim.

If you don't have a solicitor on the day of the court hearing, you may be able to obtain help from the court; some courts can appoint a 'standby' solicitor to act for you.

What to do next

When you receive the application for possession, this will give you details of the claim which your landlord is making against you. You have 14 days in which to reply on the printed form supplied with the papers. You can actually apply right up to the day of the hearing, but if your details are received so late that the court has to order an adjournment, you may be liable for costs.

On the reply form, you should write out your defence or any counterclaim you wish to make, together with details of your financial and personal circumstances. It's important that you're honest about your circumstances, which will be taken into account by the court and may count in your favour.

Your defence

Think carefully about what you're going to say on the form. Read what your landlord claims, and ask yourself if it is true. Can he prove a mandatory or discretionary ground for possession? If it's not true, perhaps you can provide evidence to challenge it successfully.

If your landlord can prove a mandatory ground, you are on shaky territory because the court *must* make an order for possession. If he's relying on a discretionary ground, even if that ground can be proved you may be able to make a case for the court suspending or postponing the order. This is where your personal and financial circumstances come in;

the court will take these into account, so it makes good sense to be full and frank about them. There may be very good reasons which would make a court reluctant to evict you.

You'll also want to check that your landlord has followed all the prescribed formalities. If he has failed to serve the right notices on you, or procedures or documents are deficient in some way, the proceedings may be thrown out by the court. Likewise, you need to have your tenancy agreement checked by an expert, to find out whether you have any security of tenure.

Making a counterclaim

Last but not least, ask yourself if you have any grounds to make a counterclaim against your landlord. Has he fulfilled all his obligations under the tenancy agreement?

Probably the commonest breach of obligations is the failure to carry out repairs and maintenance (see Chapter 6 for a more detailed look at rights and obligations). In some circumstances, it's possible to withhold rent to cover the cost of having repairs done (and your landlord may have perceived this as a failure to pay rent which is rightfully due to him). Also, there are instances where a tenant could be entitled to damages (eg for ill-health, accident, cost of repairs), which might be offset against rent arrears.

It's important to take advice on your precise situation, as your form must be correctly and fully filled in.

What if the worst happens?

Just supposing the court makes a possession order against you, and you know that you are going to lose your home - what then? It's a frightening possibility, but one which you need to think about. Taking advice early on will equip you to cope with the worst, if it happens.

Finding somewhere to live

Although there is a lot of publicity about the escalating problem of homelessness, local authorities in England and Wales do still have some obligations to house homeless people. These are contained in Part 3 of the *Housing Act 1985*. However, your local authority only has a duty to rehouse you if you meet *all* their criteria.

There are three criteria which you must meet:

1 You must be homeless or threatened with homelessness. If you are to be evicted within the next 28 days, you would usually be considered as homeless. You are 'threatened with homelessness' if your landlord has gained a court order for possession against you.

According to the rules, you are homeless if you don't have any accommodation that you are legally entitled to occupy, or if you have accommodation but can't gain access to it. You may also be classed as homeless if living in your accommodation would put you at risk of violence from someone else. If you are in temporary accommodation, such as a temporary hostel, night shelter or women's refuge, you may be classified as homeless.

2 You must be in priority need. There are several ways of satisfying this condition, for example:

- you or your partner is pregnant
- you or your partner are 'vulnerable', because of physical disability, mental handicap, mental illness, old age or some other reason
- you have dependent children living with you (or who would be living with you if you had a home)
- some kind of emergency (eg fire or flood) has made you homeless or threatened with homelessness

If you can't show that you are in priority need, you may still qualify for housing benefit - a housing advice centre or your local social security benefits office will advise you on how to make a claim.

3 You must not be intentionally homeless. This is a rather sticky one. The rules say that you are intentionally homeless if you commit some deliberate act or omission which makes you unable to occupy your existing home; or if you leave it without good reason.

There can be problems in the interpretation of this rule, but if you leave your home through a genuine mistake or ignorance of your legal rights, courts won't usually see this as a 'deliberate act or omission'.

Applying to be rehoused

If you satisfy the local authority that you have a valid claim, they must find permanent housing for you - although with the current shortage of public sector housing you could find yourself spending a long time in bed and breakfast, until suitable permanent accommodation becomes available. While your application is being considered, the authority must find suitable temporary accommodation for you.

Summing up

If possession proceedings are taken out against you, don't panic. Ask yourself if you can put up a defence to your landlord's claim, or even make a counterclaim against him.

Take advice early on; it's important that you understand your position thoroughly, and follow the set procedures carefully if you want to defend proceedings successfully, or win a counterclaim. If you qualify for legal aid, or can afford to engage a solicitor, try to have legal representation in court. If not, get as much advice as you can from housing advice centres, law centres or your CAB.

Your local social security office can supply information about your entitlement to benefits such as Housing Benefit,

Income Support and Council Tax Benefit.

Make sure that the court knows all about your financial and personal circumstances; these could be very important if a possession order is made against you.

The courts tend to be the last resort. If possible, talk to your landlord *before* small problems become big ones - particularly if you have a good, fair-minded landlord. If you think you may have trouble paying the rent, say so before you get into serious financial trouble. Take advice and put forward a possible solution. You may be able to be released from your property early, to enable you to move into a cheaper one. You may be able to share the property with another tenant. Communication is a whole lot better than confrontation.

Benefits

If you find yourself in financial difficulties, it makes sense to do some research: you may be eligible for one or more State benefits. For example, tenants on low incomes can be considered for Housing Benefit, Council Tax Benefit and/or Income Support.

The Benefits Agency and Social Security offices can supply leaflets giving information on the full range of benefits. Leaflets which you may find useful include the following:

- Income Support (leaflet IS 1)
- Family Credit (leaflet FC 1)
- How the Social Fund can help you (leaflet SFL 2)
- Help with the Council Tax (leaflet CTB 1)
- Help with your rent: Housing Benefit (leaflet RR 1)
- A guide to Housing Benefit and Council Tax Benefit (leaflet RR 2)
- Which Benefit? (leaflet FB 2) provides a useful rundown of all the benefits on offer, and who is entitled to receive them

Housing benefit

Housing Benefit is designed to help you if you have difficulty in paying your rent. The scheme is run by local councils, who award Housing Benefit for a specified period. It's sometimes called 'rent rebate' or 'rent allowance'.

Who can claim?

You don't have to be unemployed to receive Housing Benefit, and it isn't dependent on National Insurance contributions. It doesn't matter whether you are in private or public sector rented accommodation (but you can't generally claim if you're living in a residential or nursing home). If you receive Income Support and have to pay rent, you will usually get the maximum amount of Housing Benefit.

Most students don't qualify for Housing Benefit, although there are a few exceptions.

The amount you receive will depend on:

- your income
- your savings
- your personal circumstances (eg dependents)
- the amount of 'eligible rent' you pay. NB you may not receive the full amount of rent that you have to pay to your landlord, eg if it is decided that your rent is too high for the type of property you're renting, or if it is felt that the property is larger than you need for your personal circumstances

You can either make a claim at the same time as you apply for Income Support, or obtain an application form from your local council.

Council tax benefit

If there is only one adult in your home, you should be eligible to receive a discount on the amount of Council Tax you have to pay. A few people are exempt from paying Council Tax.

Who can claim?

If you need help with paying your Council Tax because you are on a low income, you can apply for Council Tax Benefit. This scheme is run by local councils.

The amount of help you receive depends on:

- your income
- your savings
- the amount of Council Tax you have to pay
- your personal circumstances

You can claim Council Tax at the same time as you apply for Income Support. Alternatively, you can obtain an application form from your local council.

Income support

If you work less than 16 hours a week, and you don't have enough money to live on, you may be able to claim Income Support. It is a benefit designed to help people on low incomes.

Who can claim?

You may be able to claim Income Support if you are:

- unemployed
- a lone parent
- in part-time work (less than 16 hours per week)
- unable to work because of sickness or disability
- 60 or over
- looking after someone who is disabled

NB Certain other people may also be able to claim, so it is worth making enquiries even if you don't fit into these categories.

Family credit

If you or your partner are working 16 or more hours per week, and have at least one child under 16 (or 19 if in full-time education), you may be able to claim Family Credit. You can obtain more information on Family Credit from your local post office or social security office.

The social fund

The Social Fund was set up to help meet expenses which are difficult to meet from your day-to-day income. It can make a grant or an interest-free loan. Your local social security office can provide additional information.

Other benefits

If you are on Income Support or have a low income, you may also be able to claim certain other benefits, eg free prescriptions, free school meals, free dental treatment, help with the cost of travelling to hospital. Leaflet AB 11 (Help with NHS Costs) contains helpful advice on health benefits.

Further information

If you would like more information about benefits, look for your local social security office in the 'phone book or Yellow Pages, under 'Benefits Agency' or 'Social Security'. Alternatively, you can contact the Citizens' Advice Bureau, or call Freeline Social Security, on **0800 666 555**, which can offer general advice about benefits.

Useful books

☼ **Benefits: the CHAR guide to means-tested benefits for single people without a permanent home**
Heather Petch (CHAR, 1995), £7.95

- **The Child Poverty Action Group rights guide to non-means-tested benefits**
  R Poynter and *C Martin* (CPAG, 1995), £6.95
- **National Welfare Benefits Handbook 1995/6**
  (CPAG, 1995), £7.95
- **Housing Associations Directory and Yearbook 1995**
  (National Federation of Housing Associations, 1995)
  Gives a clear explanation of what housing associations are, and lists housing associations by location and specialisation

Index

Need2Know Series

For further details and to order further copies, please contact

Kerrie Pateman (Editorial)
Pat Wilson (Marketing)
Need2Know
1-2 Wainman Road
Woodston
Peterborough
Cambs
PE2 7BU

Tel 01733 390801
Fax 01733 230751

Need2Know are always interested in proposals for new titles. Please contact the above address for information and a brief.

Order Information

All Need2Know titles can be ordered through your local bookshop or direct from the publisher.

____ **Help Yourself to a Job** £4.99
____ **Buying a House** £5.99
____ **Make the Most of Being a Carer** £5.99
____ **Stretch Your Money** £4.99
____ **Make the Most of Retirement** £5.99
____ **Successful Writing** £5.99
____ **Breaking Up** £5.99
____ **Superwoman** £4.99
____ **Work for Yourself and Win** £5.99
____ **The Expatriate Experience** £6.99
____ **Forget the Fear of Food** £5.99
____ **Improving your Lifestyle** £5.99

Payment Details

Please make cheques or postal orders payable to *Forward Press Ltd* adding £1 for postage and packing (if you are ordering more than three copies, postage and packing is free).

Please send orders to:

Jim Perkins
Forward Press Ltd
1-2 Wainman Road
Woodston
Peterborough
PE2 7BU
Tel: 01733 238140 Fax: 01733 230751

If you have any order queries please contact the above address.